The Confederate Blockade
of
Washington, D.C.
1861–1862

The Confederate Blockade

of

Washington, D.C.
1861–1862

Mary Alice Wills

BURD STREET PRESS

The acid-free paper used in this book meets the guidelines for permanence and durability of the Committee on Production Guidelines for Book Longevity of the Council on Library Resources.

First Printing, 1975
Second Printing, 1991
Third Printing, 1998

First Printing by
McClain Printing, Parsons, West Virginia

Second Printing by
Prince William County Historical Commission, Prince William, Virginia

Third Printing by
Burd Street Press, Shippensburg, Pennsylvania

For a complete list of available publications please write
Burd Street Press, a division of
White Mane Publishing Company, Inc.
P.O. Box 152
Shippensburg, PA 17257 USA

ISBN 1-57249-078-0 (formerly Standard Book Number 87012-200-2; Library of Congress Catalog Card Number 74-15262)

Library of Congress Cataloging-in-Publication Data

Wills, Mary Alice.
     The Confederate blockade of Washington, D.C., 1861–1862 / Mary Alice Wills.
          p.   cm.
     Originally published : Parsons, W. Va. : McClain Print. Co., [1975].
     Includes bibliographical references (p.   ) and index.
     ISBN 1-57249-078-0 (pbk. : acid-free paper)
     1. Washington (D.C.)--History--Blockade, 1861–1862. 2. Washington (D.C.)--History--Civil War, 1861–1865. 3. United States--History--Civil War, 1861–1865--Naval operations. I. Title.
E600.W55   1998
973.7'31--dc21
                                                        97-44245
                                                        CIP

PRINTED IN THE UNITED STATES OF AMERICA

FOREWORD

My first introduction to the subject of the blockade of the Potomac River by the Confederate forces early in the Civil War came as a result of a conversation with a family friend. I was intrigued with the subject because it was local history with national significance and had political, economic, and social ramifications. At the time, I was about to undertake a major research project, a graduate school dissertation, and the effect of the blockade on Washington, D.C. seemed a superbly appropriate and interesting topic. I soon discovered, however, that the blockade itself had never been adequately researched and I had to expand the project to include the military aspects as well. Since then I have pursued it through a dissertation and into this book.

Once I began serious research on the subject, I discovered that information on all phases was scattered and sketchy, particularly with regard to Confederate activities along the Potomac River. Many hours were spent researching the facts in numerous libraries, museums, and historical societies. Other libraries and museums supplied information and materials through inter-library loans. I would like to thank the staffs of the organizations listed below for the assistance which they provided in the research of this book. The principal sources of information were the National Archives and the Library of Congress. Although the staffs of all the divisions I used were helpful, I would like to thank those who provided particular assistance such as Doctor Elaine C. Everly, Old Military Branch, and Patrick D. McLaughlin, Cartographic Division of the National Archives; Charles Cooney, Manuscript Division, Library of Congress; Andrew Modelski and Thomas DeClaire, Geography and Map Division, Library of Congress.

Most of the information pertaining to the use of the balloon in southern Maryland by General Joseph Hooker's Division was found in the Air and Space Library of the Smithsonian Institution where Roger Pineau graciously provided assistance.

Detailed information on Confederate activity along the Potomac River was extremely difficult to find. I am most grateful to Colonel Harold B. Simpson, author of *Hood's Texas Brigade* and Director of the Confederate Research Center, for the material which he made available to me.

I am also indebted to the personnel of the Alexandria Library, Alexandria, Virginia; The Arlington County Public Library, Arlington, Virginia; Harold L. Eddy of The Association of American Railroads Library; The Columbia Historical Society; The Robert W. Woodruff Library for Advance Studies, Emory University; The Fairfax County Public Library, Fairfax, Virginia; Fort Ward Museum Library; Harrison Garrett of Robert Garrett and Sons for permission to use the Robert Garrett Family Papers; Ralph W. Donnelly, Assistant Head Reference Section, HGMC; Bernard R. Hensley, Hensley Gallery, Alexandria, Virginia; The Huntington Library, San Marino, California; Manassas National Battlefield Park; Richard Long, Marine Corps Museum, Quantico Marine Base; The Martin Luther King Memorial Library, Washington, D.C.; The Maryland Historical Society; The Museum of the Confederacy; The Naval Historical Foundation; The Northern Neck of Virginia Historical Society; Nellie M. Pearson, Northern Virginia Community College Library, Alexandria Campus; The Richmond, Fredericksburg and Potomac Railroad Company; Mrs. Lois Flynn, U.S. Army Heraldry Library; The U.S. Army

Library; The Southern Historical Collection, University of North Carolina Library; The Manuscript Division, University of Virginia Library; The Virginia Historical Society; and The Virginia State Library.

I am also grateful to the following individuals who have provided assistance in numerous and diverse ways: John Ashton, Doctor James W. Braden, Allen T. Carley, Alva Cohen, Howard R. Crouch, Mr. and Mrs. Richard E. Crouch, the late Edward W. Deeters, Thomas S. Dickey, Barney Dolt, Wanda Dowell, Beverly M. Dubose, Jr., James Durst, Clifton English, Harold J. Flecknoe, Brian M. Green, Thomas Hall, Richard M. Hammond, Alice C. Harmon, Frederick S. Hicks, Mark Hughes, Roger Hunt, Sydney C. Kerksis, Lewis Leigh, Jr., Jean M. Lindquist, Debbie McCray, Bryan McDonald, Edgar Milstead, Mr. and Mrs. Jesse W. Milstead, Ray A. Nolan, Stanley S. Philips, Robert Tally, Ray M. Vaden, Harry Visger, Woody West, Mr. and Mrs. Joseph E. Wills, James Wilson.

A particular debt of gratitude is owed to the following people: Roger S. Cohen, Jr., for introducing me to the subject of the blockade and for his many invaluable suggestions and criticisms; Colonel Joseph B. Mitchell, Civil War historian, who took time from his busy schedule to read the manuscript, offer constructive advice and write the preface; Eugene J. Harmon, my father, for his thorough reading of the manuscript and his many valuable suggestions; the late John T. Farrell, Ph.D., of the History Department, Catholic University, for his direction and guidance during the early stages of my research; Joseph F. Canole, Jr., for his assistance in locating sites and artifacts relating to the blockade; Robert J. Wills, my husband, to whom I am very grateful for assistance in every phase of the book including photography; and finally, to Linda and Kevin Wills who accompanied us on every field trip and who have demonstrated an interest and understanding beyond their years.

A very special added thanks is extended to Mrs. June Douglas whose last minute help made this book possible.

I would be remiss if I did not also say thank you to the many people who have expressed interest and encouragement during the years this work was being researched, compiled, and written. Most recently I also owe a thank you to the staff of White Mane Publishing Company for bringing this much in demand study back into print.

PREFACE

This book will come as a surprise to students of the Civil War, or War Between the States. Every schoolchild knows of the partial burning of Washington by the British in the War of 1812. Yet few know that, for a period of nearly five months, despite the erection of over 40 Union forts to protect the capital city, and the deployment of thousands of men and a flotilla of ships, the Confederacy cut off all access to Washington from the sea. By order of the United States Navy, ships were prohibited from attempting to use the Potomac River to bring supplies to the Capital for fear they would be destroyed by the Confederate forts and batteries blockading the river.

The *New York Tribune* called it a national disgrace and humiliation. With the other newspapers of the North, it gave the subject very limited coverage, presumably to avoid the effectiveness of the blockade from becoming a subject for common conversation.

A Southern officer wrote home describing the situation. His account was published in a local newspaper, for which he received a reprimand, although censorship was not the rule on either side. As a result, Southern newspapers of the day also avoided the issue.

Numerous historians have frequently noted the presence of Confederate forts and batteries along the Potomac, implying that they impeded and harassed Union shipping. Some writers have actually referred to these fortifications as constituting a blockade, but without explanation as to whether they were effective or not.

Now for the first time the story is told. Readers will find that Mary Alice Wills has done a remarkable amount of research in order to tell that story. Hers is a clear, candid, frequently amusing appraisal of the efforts of the military and naval forces of both sides, North and South, presented in an easy, flowing style. Accompanied by numerous photographs from many sources, it becomes a personal story, sometimes told by the participants themselves. It will appeal tremendously to anyone acquainted with this historic area, and to all others who will want to learn of this previously totally neglected phase of our country's history.

Joseph B. Mitchell

Author of *The Badge of Gallantry:*
Letters from Civil War Medal of Honor Winners

Decisive Battles of the Civil War

Military Leaders of the Civil War

CONTENTS

ILLUSTRATIONS

x

CHAPTER I

LINCOLN REFUSES TO COMPROMISE

The night train from Philadelphia was discharging its passengers. Washburne watched carefully. He had to be on that train ––– alive and well. If not . . . , no, Washburne couldn't consider the consequences; they were beyond the Congressman's imagination! Then, to his great relief, he spotted his tall lanky friend and two companions. President-elect Lincoln had arrived in Washington!

Illinois Congressman Elihu B. Washburne, Lincoln with his bodyguard, Ward Hill Lamon, and the famous detective, Allan Pinkerton, made their way to the Willard Hotel that crisp early morning of February 23, 1861. His surprise, early arrival caused the Willard management a little embarrassment because they had to move a New York businessman from their best rooms. Until his inauguration Lincoln would occupy Parlor No. 6 and its adjoining suite on the second floor overlooking Pennsylvania Avenue, "The Avenue," and the grounds of the White House.

Lincoln had been traveling with a large entourage of family, friends, politicians and military from Illinois to Washington, stopping at numerous cities for speeches and parades. His train was due to arrive in Washington on the afternoon of February 23rd and the Republicans had planned a rousing reception for their first President. The last leg of this journey, however, was fraught with danger. Lincoln's train would have to pass through the State of Maryland. Secession sympathy was so great in Maryland, that not one speaking engagement had been requested from it. Some of her military companies were openly disloyal. Congress, realizing the danger involved in the trip and inau-

1

guration, appointed a committee, composed of Congressman Washburne and Senator William Seward, in an effort to prevent violence. This committee worked very closely with General Winfield Scott, General-in-Chief of the Army, and Colonel Charles P. Stone whom Scott had entrusted with the defense of Washington. Stone had placed spies in Baltimore who reported that Baltimore gangs were planning to assassinate Lincoln as he passed through the city. Similar reports were conveyed to Pinkerton by his spies who had infiltrated the military companies and secret societies of Baltimore. Pinkerton had been employed to protect Lincoln by both his supporters in Illinois and by Samuel M. Felton, President of the Philadelphia, Wilmington and Baltimore Railroad, who also feared possible damage to his railroad by those trying to stop Lincoln. As a result of these reports General Scott concluded that Lincoln should change his plans. Senator Seward, to add emphasis to their concern, sent his son, Frederick, to Philadelphia to report the assassination rumors. The greatest danger would be in Baltimore itself. The Lincoln train would come into the city on the Philadelphia, Wilmington and Baltimore Railroad; the party would leave on the Baltimore and Ohio Railroad. As was the case in most cities, the lines were not connected and the party would have been conveyed by horse-drawn cars through hostile Baltimore from one depot to the other. By the time his party arrived, Lincoln, who had boarded the early train disguised as a sick, elderly gentleman, was safely ensconced in the Willard. He received much criticism for his secret journey and in the years following regretted having arrived in Washington in such a manner.

Staying at the Willard made Lincoln easily accessible to those many-interest groups and would-be office seekers who wanted his ear in the pre-inauguration days. One of the most important groups to meet with him was a delegation from the Peace Conference, which was holding its meetings in the Willard's concert hall, formerly the Third Presbyterian Church of Washington. The slave states of Maryland, Kentucky, Tennessee, North Carolina, Missouri, Delaware and Virginia had not followed South Carolina's secession lead in 1860 and there was still some hope that a compromise could be worked out and hos-

Willard Hotel, courtesy Library of Congress.

(3.) **THE SPECIAL TRAIN.**

"He wore a Scotch plaid Cap and a very long Military Cloak, so that he was entirely unrecognizable."

(4.) **THE OLD COMPLAINT.**

"Mr. LINCOLN, accompanied by Mr. SEWARD, paid his respects to President BUCHANAN, spending a few minutes in general conversation."

"Flight of Abraham." This cartoon is an example of the criticism Lincoln was subjected to for his secret arrival in Washington prior to his inauguration. *Harper's Weekly,* March 9, 1861.

tilities avoided. Ex-President John Tyler of Virginia, Chairman of the Conference, and Senator Salmon P. Chase, Democrat turned Republican, led the delegation to Parlor No. 6. On the slave issue Lincoln refused to compromise. He flatly rejected the Crittenden Amendment which would have prohibited slavery in territories north of 36°30′, protected it south of that line and allowed future states north or south of that line to enter the Union, slave or free, as they chose. He had run on a Republican Party platform opposing the extension of slavery in the territories. On principle he would not compromise even though it might possibly have averted war.

Many of the Southern representatives to the Conference returned home with their disheartening news. Virginia was the key state; it had taken the lead in calling the Peace Conference and its course would more than likely determine whether or not a Confederacy would be strong enough to make a stand against the Federal Government for independence. The Virginia Convention had been deliberating an ordinance of secession from mid-February. Approval seemed imminent.

Southerners began their exodus from Washington on the heels of the Peace delegates. Maids and servants packed the trunks and boxes and piled the baggage wagons high. Houses were locked; hotel rooms vacated. A society made its way over the bumpy roads to the steamers bound for Aquia Creek.

Southwest Washington, which was separated from other sections of the city by the old canal, was often referred to as the Island. Among the buildings located there were the Smithsonian Institution, the U. S. Arsenal, which is currently the site of Fort McNair, and the Penitentiary. At the foot of Sixth and Seventh Streets were the city's main wharves. It was here that the steamers and sailing vessels which connected Washington with the rest of the country, Europe and South America unloaded their goods. Washington, it must be remembered, was a port city. It was here also that the steamboats connecting Washington with the railroad at Aquia Creek, Virginia, docked and where, at the end of February, 1861, Southern baggage was piling up waiting to be loaded.

The most direct route to all points south was the Washington to Richmond route. Richmond was serviced by five railroads which connected it with other important southern cities. The trip to Richmond was via steamboat and rail. Travelers boarded the ships in Washington and made the 3½ hour trip down the Potomac River to Aquia Creek. At that point was located the depot of the Richmond, Fredericksburg and Potomac Railroad, a direct line with Richmond about 75 miles and 5½ hours away.

Prior to 1815 travel to Washington from points south was entirely by stage, 38 hours from Richmond with a stopover in Fredericksburg. The time was gradually reduced, first by connecting the stage route with boat service at Potomac Creek and Aquia Creek and then by a sectional building of the R. F. & P. with stagecoaches running the remainder of the route to the Potomac. In 1842, the R. F. & P. was completed to Aquia Creek and the Washington & Fredericksburg Steamboat Co. took passengers the rest of the way. Three years later, to provide well-coordinated service between Richmond and Washington, the R. F. & P. purchased one-half of the capital stock of the steamboat company, and its officers were elected officers and directors of the W. & F. Steamboat Co. Under this arrangement the steamboat company got one-fourth of the gross receipts from all through passengers, mail and freight traffic to and from the railroad, as well as all revenue from passengers traveling on the boats and from all meals served on the boats. In 1855, the name of the Washington & Fredericksburg Steamboat Co. was changed to the Potomac Steamboat Co. In 1861, there were four steamboats plying the Potomac taking the Southerners home—the *Powhatan, Mount Vernon, Baltimore* and *Maryland.*

Former President John Tyler presided over the Peace Conference which was held in the concert hall of the Willard Hotel. Courtesy Library of Congress.

R.F.&P. train starting out from 8th and Broad Streets, Richmond, Virginia. Courtesy Virginia State Library.

CHAPTER II

THE WAR BEGINS

Inauguration day soon arrived. Perhaps more nervous even than Abraham Lincoln was "Old Fuss and Feathers," Winfield Scott, famed veteran of the Mexican War and unsuccessful Whig Presidential candidate in 1852. He was 74 years old in 1861, with so many infirmities he was unable to sit on a horse, but he was still the General-in-Chief of the Army; and the safety of Washington and of the new President were his responsibility. There were many rumors that secession sympathizers would riot to disrupt the inaugural ceremonies and perhaps even make an attempt on Lincoln's life. Scott and Stone stationed loyal troops at strategic places around the Capitol just in case. But the day passed quietly and the old General took his weary bones home for a good night's rest.

President James Buchanan's policy toward the seceded states had been one of inaction. By the time Lincoln took over the reins of government all important forts and navy yards in the rebellious states except Fort Pickens at Pensacola and Fort Sumter at Charleston had fallen into Confederate hands. The first month of Lincoln's administration was also marked by inaction but for different reasons. He had his eye on Virginia. Some of the most capable officers in the U. S. Army were from the Old Dominion, there was a strong Union sentiment as noted in Virginia's voting for Bell rather than Breckinridge in the 1860 election, her soil was sure to be a battleground and her convention still had not voted to leave the Union. And also, with Virginia in the Union a reconciliation might have been possible with those states that had already seceded. If Virginia seceded, North Carolina, Kentucky, Tennessee, Missouri, Arkansas and Maryland would probably follow.

By the beginning of April it became apparent that Fort Sumter, for both sides, had become a matter of principle. If civil war broke out, it would be of no strategic value to the North. Yet, the Confederacy had made it clear that any attempt to reinforce it would be regarded as an act of war. Major Robert Anderson, in charge of defending the harbor fortification, notified the War Department that his supplies were exceedingly low and that Confederate batteries commanded his position. In spite of supplications by Confederate Commissioners in Washington and entreaties by General Scott to let the "Wayward Sisters depart in peace," Lincoln decided to provision the fort. To yield on Sumter would be to yield on the principle of union. Virginia would have to accept federalism as it was or accept the consequences.

For Jefferson Davis, Fort Sumter was a means to an end. He needed a collision with Federal authorities to fire the Southern spirit and bring the fence-sitting Virginians into the Confederate camp. He ordered General P.G.T. Beauregard, former superintendent of West Point, Commander of the Charleston District, to fire on Fort Sumter if an attempt was made to re-supply it. Anderson had refused an invitation to surrender. Early on April 12th the batteries opened fire on Sumter. The relief expedition which appeared off the fort was unable to prevent its fall. The Civil War had begun!

Any hope of compromise was then shattered. Jefferson Davis and the provisional government at Montgomery won a clear cut victory. The Southern conspiracy had become a full fledged revolution. On Monday, April 15, 1861, the following proclamation was issued by the President of the United States:

> Whereas, the laws of the United States have been for some time past and now are opposed, and the execution thereof obstructed in the States of South Carolina, Georgia, Alabama, Florida, Mississippi, Louisiana and Texas by combinations too powerful to be suppressed by the ordinary course of judicial proceedings, or by the powers vested in the marshals by law: now . . . , I, Abraham Lincoln, President

Inauguration of President Lincoln, March 1861. *Harper's Weekly*,
March 16, 1861.

> of the United States, in virtue of the power in-
> vested in me by the Constitution and the laws,
> have thought it fit to call forth, and thereby
> do call forth the militia of the several States
> of the Union, to the aggregate number of sev-
> enty-five thousand, in order to suppress said
> combinations and to cause the laws to be duly
> executed.

The die was cast; it was up to the Border States to take their stand. Virginia, the most influential state, elected the Confederacy. On April 17, 1861, in secret session, the Virginia Convention passed an ordinance of secession, 88-55. A pretense was made of submitting the question to a popular vote on May 23, 1861. The outcome was a foregone conclusion. By then Governor John Letcher had called out the militia, seized the U.S. Navy Yard at Norfolk and the U.S. Armory at Harper's Ferry, and entered into an agreement with the Confederate States. North Carolina, Tennessee and Arkansas followed the Old Dominion's lead.

The decision of Maryland was critical to the defense of the Capital. Washington, D.C., was located between Maryland and Virginia, a geographically perilous position. If Maryland seceded, the Capital of the United States would be isolated within the boundaries of the rebellious states. It could conceivably become the capital of the Confederate States of America! To the South, the capture of Washington would be a supreme accomplishment which would enhance its prestige and perhaps bring it recogni- tion by England and France. To the North, Washington was a symbol of the nation's power. Unlike Paris or London, which were industrial and cultural centers, Washington had no signifi- cance other than being the political capital, the nerve center of the nation. But that alone meant its defense was a national priority—Washington was to be defended at any cost.

Securing Maryland in the Union, therefore, was essential. Only then could Washington's arms of communication and trans- portation with the North and foreign countries be maintained. The principal route of communication and supply was the Po- tomac River, one bank of which was in rebel hands. The other shore was contiguous to Charles County and St. Marys County, Maryland. Both were notoriously sympathetic with the Southern cause, regularly communicated with Virginia, and sent many of their sons to join the rebel army. The other link with the North was by rail, a forty mile branch of the Baltimore and Ohio Railroad, which connected Washington with Baltimore and other railroads north.

Maryland was really a microcosm of the nation's problems with a warring population torn between the Union and the Confederacy. On April 19th some of her citizens even attacked the 6th Massachusetts Regiment as it passed between depots in Baltimore. It was on its way to Washington in response to President Lincoln's call for troops. Baltimore officials, with the cooperation of Governor Thomas Hicks, approved severing the railroad lines leading into the city from the north and banning all troops from the city's streets. This order temporarily cut Washington's rail link with the North.

President Lincoln did not want to take a hard-nosed stand on the issue of Union troops marching through Baltimore. A series of conferences was held between state officials and the War Department which resulted in an altered plan of march. Troops were to be sent to Perryville at the mouth of the Susquehanna River. From there they would be ferried to Annapolis and embarked on the Annapolis and Elk Ridge Railroad for an eighteen mile trip to Annapolis Junction where they would meet the Baltimore and Ohio to Washington. The route was protected by Federal troops.

In April, 1861, it appeared that Maryland's anti-Union voice was that of the majority and that secession was imminent. President Lincoln was concerned about Maryland's fate considering the strong anti-Union activity in Baltimore. For a time historians felt that only the quick presence of Federal troops in Maryland as well as Lincoln's suspension of the habeas corpus and the moving of the state legislature to Frederick saved the state for the Union. By the end of April, 1861, there were indications that tempers were beginning to cool. More recent investigation of the issue has indicated that left on its own Maryland would not have seceded. The majority of her citizens were pro-North and the more moderate of the pro-Southerners came to the conclusion that it was in Maryland's best interest as a state to side with the Union because of its geography. Maryland's decision to remain loyal meant that Washington, D.C., was geographically part of the North and not an island in the midst of rebellion. Of the other border states Kentucky, Missouri, and the western sector of Virginia remained within the Union.

CHAPTER III

ESTABLISHMENT OF THE POTOMAC FLOTILLA

After Virginia's secession and the Baltimore riots, Washington saw another exodus from the city. Women, children, Southern politicians who had elected not to follow the Peace Delegates home, and pro-Southern military officers such as Commodore Franklin Buchanan, Commander of the Washington Navy Yard, who resigned U.S. Commissions in favor of ones from the C.S.A. left Washington. But they no longer had an easy route home. On April 19th the four steamboats of the Potomac Steamboat Co. serving the R.F. & P. at Aquia Creek were seized in Washington by the U.S. government and appropriated for use as Federal transports and naval vessels. Not only did that interfere with transportation south, it also deprived the State of Virginia of the ships for possible naval duty, perhaps as a rebel flotilla on the Potomac.*

Washington abounded in rumors, some utterly fantastic, some quite plausible. One reached the ears of General Winfield Scott on April 22nd. Along the Potomac River there are numerous promontories which would easily lend themselves to fortification. From their side of the river, the Virginians could harass Union shipping and with guns of sufficient caliber could even close the river to traffic. The Potomac in the early months of the war teemed with shipping of all sorts; large ocean going steamers, coastal freighters, army and navy transports, fishing and oyster boats, as well as local river traffic. Rumors were heard in Washington that the Virginians were building a battery on White House Point (also known as White Stone Point), four miles below Mount Vernon. A party from the U.S.S. *Anacostia* under Lieutenant Thomas Scott Fillebrown examined the point

---

*The Potomac Steamboat Co. later received $170,000 in compensation from the United States for the seizures.

on April 28th and found no signs of any force having been there. In accordance with the directive from Gideon Welles, the Secretary of the Navy, that a close watch be kept on the important points along the Potomac, White House Point was regularly checked. Assisting the *Anacostia* in the chore was the U.S.S. *Pawnee,* a regular sloop-of-war with twin screws, eight 9-inch guns and two 12-pounders. To the great relief of official Washington, no evidence of a battery was ever found at the point.

This only proved that there was no immediate danger on the Potomac. It didn't rule out a future day or week; and the seriousness of the threat was enough to have elicited a personal directive to the Navy from the President. The *Pawnee* would have challenged the battery if one existed on White House Point but a few ships could never keep the Potomac open if the Virginians decided to fortify various points along the shore. A sizable force was needed to patrol the river. President Lincoln's Proclamation of April 27, 1861, partially remedied the situation by extending the blockade of the Southern states to include Virginia and North Carolina. In accordance with that order, the Potomac Flotilla was established at the Washington Navy Yard in May. At first it was part of the Atlantic Blockading Squadron but due to its distance from the flagship, it quickly became independent. Commander James Harmon Ward, U.S. Navy, was selected by Gideon Welles, the Secretary of the Navy, to be the Flotilla Commander. Ward, who was born in 1806 in Hartford, Connecticut, was an experienced naval officer having served in the Mediterranean squadron off the coast of Africa and in the Gulf of Mexico. Sixteen years of his career were spent at sea; nine on shore which included a teaching position at the U.S. Naval Academy at Annapolis. Prior to his assuming command of the Potomac Flotilla, he commanded the *North Carolina* stationed at the New York Naval Yard.

For his flagship Ward chose the *Thomas Freeborn*, a converted New York side-wheel steam ferryboat which was armed with two 32-pounder guns. Other ships of the Flotilla included the small screw steamers, *Reliance* and *Resolute*. Both carried a 24-pounder and a 12-pound howitzer. The *Anacostia* was a twin-screw sloop and carried two 9-inch Dahlgren smooth bores.

The screw sloop *Pocahontas* had six guns. Another ship, the *Mount Vernon,* a side-wheel steamer with one gun, was one of the four ships of the Potomac Steamboat Co. seized at Washington. The *Pawnee,* under Commander S. C. Rowan, the best vessel on the Potomac, was also detailed to the Flotilla. The purpose of the Potomac Flotilla was twofold. It was to restrict communication between insurgents on the Virginia and Maryland shores and keep the water approach to Washington open. Ward immediately began patrolling the Potomac. His chief point of rendezvous and supply was Nanjemoy Creek, Charles County, Maryland. The home port, of course, was the Washington Navy Yard.

United States Steamer *Pawnee*. (O. R. Navies.)

The Washington Navy Yard with shad fishing in the foreground.
Harper's Weekly, April 20, 1861.

CHAPTER IV

AQUIA CREEK

Washington's population had been apprehensive about a war but the feeling was allayed with the influx of soldiers. War greatly improved business. Barbers, vendors, restaurateurs were delighted; sutlers moved into vacant shops. Troops, encamped throughout the city, held parades, drills, and concerts. It was like a holiday!

At the docks the ships never stopped coming. Steamers, schooners, packets, and tugs came loaded to capacity with government orders—tents, cots, blankets, uniforms, cooking utensils, provisions, arms, horses, cattle, wagons, and even reels of insulated wire for the telegraph. The railroad station, likewise, was very busy.

None of this activity was kept secret from the Virginians. Newspapers, spy reports, correspondence, and supplies were transported from southern Maryland to Virginia each night. From their vantage point on the bank of the Potomac, they were aware of the hundreds of ships going up the river with supplies for the Union Army organizing in Washington. It did not take long for the Virginians to realize that the most immediate opportunity for harassing the Union, and perhaps even strangling Washington, rested along that line. They also realized that a Union attack could come via the Potomac. A landing on the Virginia shore to secure the Potomac or to take the R. F. and P. depot were possibilities that had to be considered. It should also be noted that Virginia was not formally part of the Confederacy at that time. Therefore, all its military activity was under the control of Governor Letcher. On May 7

View of the Sixth Street wharf, Washington, D.C., 1863. Courtesy Library of Congress.

Virginia was admitted as a state into the Confederacy. The state's action was affirmed by the plebiscite of May 23rd and Richmond became the Confederate capital. Responsibility for military activities in the state was shifted to Jefferson Davis and the Confederate government on June 6th.

The thought of a battery on the Potomac continued to disturb General Scott. When the first one appeared, it was not at White House Point as expected but rather at Aquia Creek, well below White House. Shortly after the seizure of the steamboats by the Federal Government, the State of Virginia took possession of the R. F. and P. Railroad property at Aquia for military purposes. Command of the Potomac line, which extended from Mount Vernon to the mouth of the Rappahannock River, was given by the Governor of Virginia to Daniel Ruggles. He was a native of Massachusetts who resigned his commission from the U.S. Army on May 7th and went to Richmond where Governor Letcher commissioned him a Brigadier General of Virginia Volunteers. His command was known as the Department of Fredericksburg, with headquarters at Fredericksburg. It is quite probable that his marriage connections there inspired him to join the Southern cause.

One of Ruggles' first official actions was to order an examination of Aquia Creek with a view to fortifying it. If the Union effected a successful landing there, they would have a direct rail approach to Fredericksburg via the R. F. and P. Also located there were railroad irons and timber, two small vessels, and a steamer, the *George Page.*

Major Thomas H. Williamson of the Virginia Army Engineers and Lieutenant Hunter H. Lewis, Virginia Navy, undertook the task on April 24th. After examining the topography of the land and its relation to the Potomac River channel, they recommended the construction of a battery on Split Rock Bluff which was on the same side of the creek as the railroad, and could, therefore, protect the R. F. & P. facilities as well as guard the vessels docked there. Heavy guns would have the added advantage of being close enough to the Potomac River to be able to command the channel. The alternative site was Brent's Point, on the opposite side of Aquia Creek, the right hand side as one enters the creek from the Potomac. A battery there would invite an attack and be hard to hold. They recommended that a small force of ten to twenty men be kept there to fend off enemy boats.

Captain William F. Lynch, Commander of the Naval Defenses on the Potomac, whose job was to examine the defensible points on the river, also reviewed Aquia Creek. He regarded a battery at Aquia as highly desirable but specified it should be designed to protect the avenues of approach to the railway terminal not to command the Potomac River channel. The vessels were of secondary importance. Based on Lynch's report plus those of Williamson and Lewis, Major General Robert E. Lee instructed General Ruggles to proceed with the construction of a battery. He left the exact spot for it and the disposition of troops up to Ruggles' discretion, stipulating only that the defense of the railroad and general protection of the country be the main considerations.

On May 8th, the battery was located not on Split Rock Bluff but at the Railroad Landing. Major Thomas H. Williamson was in charge of its construction; operation of it fell to the Navy. In the absence of Captain Lynch, Commander Robert D. Thornburn was directed by Ruggles to put the guns in position.

Because it was difficult to get men to volunteer for naval duty even for a shore battery, the gun crews consisted of volunteers from Fredericksburg and from Stafford, Caroline and Spotsylvania Counties. The guns for the battery, two of which are believed to have been among those captured in the United States Navy Yard at Norfolk, Virginia, were sent to Aquia by General Lee. During the evenings the Confederates methodically destroyed the buoys and channel markers on the Potomac making navigation difficult for those unfamiliar with the channel.

Although the Virginia shore was carefully watched by Ward's Flotilla, the Aquia battery went undetected for a week.

Ironically, the ship which carried Lieutenant J. Glendy Sproston into Aquia to discover the battery was the *Mount Vernon,* one of the four steamers of the Potomac Steamboat Company that carried passengers from Aquia Creek to Washington before it was seized by the U.S. Government in April.

At daylight on May 14th Sproston steamed into Aquia Creek and stopped about one third of a mile off from the wharf. He took out his glass and focused on the shore. Staring him back was a 32-pounder trained right on the *Mount Vernon.* It was one of four guns mounted in a semi-circular earthern battery with four embrasures. While Sproston watched, some trees which partially shielded the battery were felled. About fifty men, some in uniform and some carrying muskets were in and about the battery.

After about ten minutes Sproston backed the *Mount Vernon* around and steamed out of Aquia Creek. No shots were fired. The little single-gunned ship could not possibly have made a good showing against the guns observed in the battery, the first to be discovered on the Potomac.

The senior officers at Aquia were not present when the *Mount Vernon* steamed into the creek. Lieutenant George H. Peyton, who was commanding the battery at the time, withheld the order to fire biding time for his messenger to return with reinforcements. By the time they arrived, the ship was gone.

The *Fredericksburg Recorder* expressed disappointment that there was no engagement and Stafford County offered to supply "six foot farms for forty-thousand Yankees." The *Anacostia,* which docked at the Navy Yard on May 18th, brought word of the batteries to the Commandant, John A. Dahlgren, inventor of the Dahlgren gun. Lieutenant Sproston returned to Aquia on the 19th. Three new guns were mounted in the battery. On the 24th Lieutenant William Jeffers of the U.S.S. *Philadelphia* noticed a secession flag flying at Aquia Creek as he passed by.

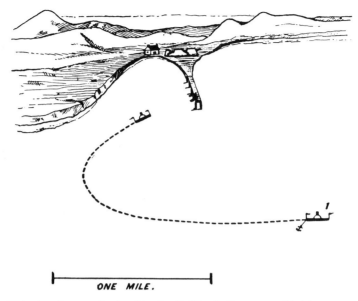

ONE MILE.

This sketch was submitted by Lt. J. Glendy Sproston with his report on the battery at Aquia Creek Landing which he discovered on May 14, 1861. (O. R. Navies.)

Requisition for stationery by Capt. W. B. Fitzgerald, C.S.N., stationed at Battery No. 1, Aquia Creek. Courtesy National Archives.

No shots were exchanged between the battery and the Flotilla until the end of May. The main concern on the part of the Confederates was that the Union Army and Navy would attempt a landing at Aquia and capture the railroad which provided a direct route to Fredericksburg. There were standing orders from headquarters in Richmond that if such an event occurred the facilities at Aquia Creek and the railroad as far along the line as possible should be destroyed.

The Union was not contemplating a landing at that time. It was too early in the war. To try the battery and determine its strength Ward initiated a mild engagement on the evening of the 29th but it was ineffective. The tide was out and he was unable to get the *Freeborn* in close enough. One man on the Confederate side was slightly wounded in the hand by a shell fragment; no Union injuries were reported.

Hearing of the engagement and fearing it meant a Union landing, Ruggles rushed by train from Fredericksburg with seven hundred men from the 2nd Tennessee Regiment and a battalion of volunteers. By the time they arrived, the engagement had ended. Ruggles returned with his men to Fredericksburg.

On May 30th Commander Ward, with a party of seamen, landed on Mathias Point downriver and satisfied himself that no batteries existed. The next morning Ward was back at Aquia Creek ready for another encounter—the first significant battle of the Civil War between the U.S. Navy and batteries of a rebel state. The *Thomas Freeborn* was supported by the *Anacostia* and the *Resolute* in an engagement which lasted two to three hours. The ships withdrew when all their ammunition for distant firing was expended. During the exchange the guns at the railroad landing were silenced. Another battery, however, Captain John S. Walker's field battery of four 3-inch rifled guns was established on the heights in the rear of the original one. It was under the immediate command of Lieutenant Patton Robertson, a volunteer from Tennessee. For nearly an hour it hailed shots on and around the ships. Although the damage was slight, one sailor was wounded. The ships were helpless against the new battery because they could not elevate their guns high enough to reach it. Ward had the *Reliance* and *Reso-lute* stay out of range for want of a rifled gun.

Ward was very happy with the action that day despite the field battery. He was particularly proud of the new gun carriages, of his own design, which were on the *Freeborn.* They had a sweep of 140° which enabled the ships to maneuver without interrupting the gunners.

On shore two shots from the *Anacostia* exploded in a sand-bank. One of them completely demolished the room occupied by Captain Lynch and his officers. For some inexplicable reason, no one was injured. Again, when appraised of the conflict, General Ruggles took his force to Aquia and once again arrived too late. This time, however, he left the Tennessee Legion, also known as Walker's Legion, under Colonel William B. Bate, at Brooke Station, close to Aquia Creek. In addition to the disappointment of arriving at Aquia too late, Ruggles received a reprimand from the Governor for allowing forces under his command to respond to the attack. Letcher thought the engagements "could have no other result than to waste ammunition and to expose our condition and the strength of the batteries, which was probably the object of his visit."

In his official report to Gideon Welles, Secretary of the Navy, Commander Ward said that he doubted it was possible "to reduce the batteries now established on the heights from ships; nor is it at all important, considering that they are remote from the ship channel of the river and command only the railroad terminus." He must have had second thoughts that evening; his actions the next day contradicted the report. He returned to Aquia Creek and resumed the battle.

The *Anacostia* and *Reliance* accompanied the *Freeborn* to Aquia but were directed not to go within range of the Confederate guns. They were to stand by and be prepared for rescue duty if necessary. Accompanying the *Freeborn* into action was the *Pawnee* with its many guns. The latter had re-supplied the *Freeborn* during the evening. The bombardment began at 11:30 a.m. with the *Freeborn* leading the *Pawnee* onto the scene. As they approached within range of the battery, the Confederates set fire to the building at the extreme end of the wharf. This was done at the direction of Captain Lynch who was convinced, though mistakenly so, that the Lincoln gunners were using the end of the wharf to sight upon the battery. He therefore had the furniture and other contents moved to the rear of the battery and the building fired. Ward thought it must have presented an obstruction to the rebel gunners' aim. The fire burned for the duration of the engagement; only charred piles were left above the water. The Richmond, Fredericksburg and Potomac Railroad later estimated the loss at $11,200.

The confrontation was between the ships and the battery at the railroad landing—Naval Battery No. I. It is sometimes referred to in the plural because of the numerous embrasures. The battery on the heights, Walker's, was gone. One of Walker's guns under the command of Lieutenant Robertson was moved down to the Naval Battery. There appeared to be at least eight guns, possibly more, under the direct command of Captain Lynch. The three other guns and the remainder of Colonel Bate's Walker's Legion were in reserve ready to prevent a landing if one was attempted. Occasionally some of the Tennessee men ventured from concealment for a better view of the fight and became the target of a sailor's gun.

Twice during the five hour engagement the batteries were silenced. Over five hundred rounds of ammunition were fired by the *Freeborn* and *Pawnee*. The batteries expended much fewer. Lynch was careful to fire only when a fair shot presented itself. The gunners had to fire through embrasures which necessitated waiting for the ships to come within range. In addition, Lynch wanted to conserve ammunition. He did not know how long the June 1st conflict would last or if his supply of ammunition could be replenished quickly enough if he were subjected to a series of cannonades by the Flotilla.

By 4 p.m. the Confederates had abandoned most of their positions. A single gun was still in use but was being fired at long intervals. Ward, who did not want to wear his men out on "so feeble a fire," as the day was very hot, discontinued the en-

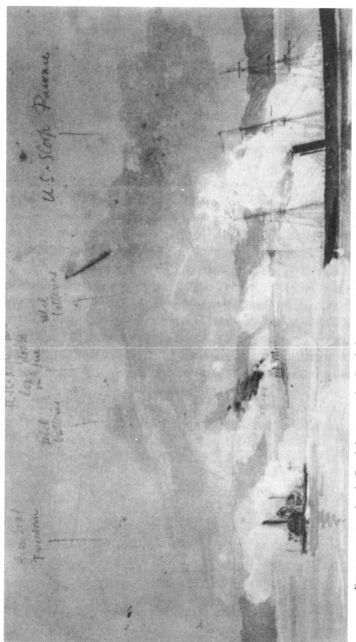

Engagement at Aquia Creek between the Confederate naval battery and ships of the Potomac Flotilla, June 1, 1861. Courtesy Library of Congress.

gagement at 4:30. Ruggles, who had arrived too late for the prior two conflicts, made it to Aquia in time to witness about three hours of the action.

Both the *Freeborn* and *Pawnee* were damaged. Several shots hit the *Freeborn* causing her to leak badly and crippling the port wheel. No one was killed or wounded. The *Pawnee* was hit nine times. Four shots hit the hull. One of them passed through the bulwarks and tore up part of the deck. Those that hit above the hull damaged the maintopsail, mizzenmast, and the first cutter. There were no casualties; Captain Craven received the only wound, a slight scratch on the face from a splinter. The *Anacostia* and *Reliance* which stayed out of range were not hit.

On the Confederate side, in addition to the wharf which burned, the earthworks were damaged, the buildings behind the battery were destroyed and the railroad track torn up in three or four places. A chicken and a horse were killed but according to Lynch "thanks to a kind Providence, who seems to smile benignly upon our cause, no one with us was injured."

Ward proceeded to Washington to get the *Freeborn* repaired and to refill the ship's magazines. The *Pawnee*, which was more serviceable, took over the *Freeborn*'s cruising ground. When the flagship returned to the Potomac, the *Pawnee* put in for repairs.

On shore it was not realized that the Flotilla was too crippled to renew the engagement. The Confederates expected the ships to return for another round, perhaps with a landing party. By 5 p.m. the Confederates were hard at work repairing the damaged naval battery and establishing new ones. By morning June 2nd they were ready for an attack. In addition to the naval battery, a new one was constructed on a steep hill consisting of two heavy columbiads and garrisoned by the Carolina Greys. It was expected that its guns would also reach the Potomac. Captain Walker's guns with two rifle companies of Walker's Legion were ready on the opposite side of Aquia Creek at the tip of Brent's Point. The Flotilla, however, never arrived.

The rebels were disappointed. Colonel Bate said "the arrangement Sunday morning (June 2) would have sunk their ships in an hour had they resumed their positions."

The reprieve gave both sides an opportunity to ponder the significance of the engagements. Neither side could claim victory. Yet, neither side felt defeat. Ward was satisfied that the Aquia Creek guns would not be a threat to traffic on the Potomac River and that they could be silenced by the *Pawnee's* heavy guns if it were desirable. The Confederates were sure that they would be able, particularly with more batteries, to meet an attack and prevent a landing. On June 11, 1861, Colonel William B. Bate wrote Mr. L. P. Walker, Confederate Secretary of War, "I foresee skirmishes at Aquia Creek from now on but nothing more. We will sink their ships in another effort if they come in range." By the 15th the Confederates had 12 guns in position. Governor Letcher was also confident that the batteries at the Creek together with the force in the Fredericksburg area could repulse a Union landing. According to John Dowling, who deserted from the Confederate Navy at Aquia Creek on June 21st, there were three thousand men encamped behind the hills, forty-two men at the depot and three batteries, the naval battery and two on the hills. He said that the steamer *Page* was neither manned nor armed.

The Potomac River off Aquia Creek became the cruising ground for the *Pawnee.* Any other ships of the Flotilla could have kept a close eye on Confederate activities and observed the construction of new batteries; for example one on Brent's Point at the mouth of Aquia and a second one on a hill about a mile behind the landing. But only the *Pawnee* could reckon with the *George Page.* Even if the steamer were unarmed, the other ships of the Flotilla were considered too small to be able to fend off a surprise boarding attempt which the rebels could conceivably attempt on a dark or foggy night with the aid of the *Page.* Ward did not wish to risk letting an armed naval vessel fall into rebel hands. Also, if the ship guarding the creek were captured, it would temporarily free the river for communication between the Virginia and Maryland shores long enough possibly to give the rebels an opportunity to cross in force into southern Maryland.

If the *George Page* were armed and allowed to run out of Aquia Creek, it would create a menace to river traffic. It was felt that the *Pawnee* with its many heavy guns would be in a better position to prevent the *Page*'s escape than any other member of the Flotilla.

No other engagements of the May 31st or June 1st scale occurred at Aquia Creek. Ships at times shelled the batteries and the batteries sometimes fired at the ships. The guns, however, were too remote from the channel of the Potomac River to interfere with the transportation of goods and troops to and from Washington. Aquia Creek was a menace but not a threat to Potomac traffic.

It should be noted that some important changes occurred in Virginia in the early part of June. On the 5th, Brigadier General Theophilus H. Holmes of North Carolina relieved Ruggles as Commander of the Department of Fredericksburg. Holmes made his headquarters at Brooke Station; Ruggles remained at Fredericksburg in a subordinate capacity. On June 6th command of the military forces in the state was formally shifted from the Governor of Virginia to the authorities of the Confederate States of America.

Quarterdeck of the *Pawnee* and the starboard battery. *The Photographic History of the Civil War.*

Invoice of ordnance and ordnance Stores belonging to the State of Virginia Dept of Fredericksburg turned over by Col D Ruggles Prov. Army to Capt R S Chew Commanding Co B volunteers Fredericksburg Va Viz. */May 31. 1861*

1000   One thousand Cartridges with Caps

I certify on honor that the above ordnance and ordnance Stores have been sent to Capt Chew while on service at Acquia O

Daniel Ruggles
Colonel ... Army
... ...

Invoice for 1,000 cartridges and caps sent to Captain Chew at Aquia Creek. It is signed by General Daniel Ruggles.

CHAPTER V

MATHIAS POINT

U. S. Government authorities were surprised when the first rebel battery appeared at Aquia Creek. There were many other points along the river better suited for shore batteries. White House Point, a constant concern, was the closest to Washington. The boldest promontory on the Potomac was some 18 miles below Aquia Creek in King George County, Virginia. Mathias Point, covered with woods and brush, and 20 feet above the water, forced the Potomac to take a sharp, short turn bringing a very narrow channel close to shore. Also, the opposite shore was 4,000 yards away which precluded the possibility of silencing batteries from Maryland.

Early in May, Captain Lynch made a reconnaissance of the Potomac to determine the defensible points which would "prevent northern navigation of the Potomac." Mathias Point was one. On the 4th of May, at his direction, Major Thomas H. Williamson, the engineer, checked it out. Williamson sent a detailed report of his examination to General Ruggles. "To prevent the enemy from passing up the Potomac" he recommended a "semi-circular sunken battery on the side next to the river with ten heavy guns and an entrenchment on the land side." There was no doubt that a strong battery there could close the river. But the wisdom of constructing one was challenged by Captain Lynch. He pointed out the necessity for supporting it with a force larger than General Ruggles had at his disposal. General Robert E. Lee, consequently, directed that guns marked for Mathias Point be sent to Aquia Creek to guard the approaches to Fredericksburg. Entrenchment was postponed until everything needed for the battery was on the point, with a sufficient number of troops for its protection.

The Navy Department was also aware of its vulnerability at that point. On May 30, 1861, Commander Ward, accompanied by Acting Master Budd, Master's Mate Lee and a party of seamen made a minute exploration of Mathias Point covering an area 300 yards wide and 3 miles long. No indications of a battery were found. They were convinced, however, that it was the most dangerous point on the river. Little did they know this realization was not theirs alone.

Confederate forces were detailed to Mathias Point. One of the first companies to arrive was the Farmer's Fork Grays from Richmond County. They were mustered into service on the 4th of June and arrived at the point on the 10th. Sergeant James M. Scates has left us an account of their activity until the Regiment was transferred on the 29th. There were other troops stationed there as well, under the command of Colonel J. M. Brockenbrough of the 40th Virginia Volunteers.

All was quiet until the 15th when the schooner *Christina Keen* went aground on the Virginia shore. About 30 cavalry from the Farmer's Fork Grays boarded and burned the vessel off Hooe's Ferry, just below Mathias Point. The ship had been trying to navigate at night in an area of the river almost devoid of markers. In retaliation, Budd of the *Resolute* first shelled and then landed and burned the beautiful home of Doctor A. B. Hooe. Hooe, who was an active Southern patriot, not only owned boats engaged in carrying contraband across the Potomac, but also had converted his schoolhouse and outbuildings into barracks for twenty-five men.

On the 17th the Farmer's Fork Grays fired on a passing tug. The same day General Lee directed General Holmes to construct a battery on Mathias Point if the increased force there was sufficient to protect it and prevent a Yankee landing. On the 20th he rescinded the order having determined that Holmes' force was not strong enough. But he added, "I desire you to keep its establishment in view, as it is proposed to place one there when circumstances will permit." Lee also ordered the troops to stop shooting at ships and to keep themselves concealed so as, "not to attract enemy attention."

This activity seemed to indicate to Commander Ward that Mathias Point was being fortified by the Confederates. Presuming that General Scott would provide the necessary assistance, Ward requested through the Navy Department two hundred soldiers to denude the point of the jungle that made observation so difficult. Dahlgren and Gideon Welles took the letter to General Scott. "A battalion! He shall have two!" was his reply. After a pause and a second thought, Scott backed down. Dahlgren would have to take it up with General Joseph Mansfield, Commander of the Department of Washington. General Mansfield was hesitant and called a conference to discuss it the next day.

The meeting was attended by General Mansfield, Major John G. Barnard and Captain Daniel P. Woodbury, Army Engineers, and Captain William Palmer, Topographical Engineer, as well as Dahlgren. All of the soldiers opposed the action, suspecting that a large Confederate force might be stationed there. As an alternative, they agreed to send Woodbury and Palmer to make a reconnaissance. They left from the Navy Yard at 3 p.m., June 24th, on board the *Pawnee.*

In the wee hours of the next morning the *Pawnee* stood off Mathias Point and began shelling it. The Confederates were sent scurrying. Many narrowly missed being killed when one bomb shell passed through the house in which thirty men of the Farmer's Fork Grays were camped. Luckily only one man was in the house at the time. The same shell then burst outside near a spring where twenty-five men had gathered. One man was slightly hurt by a small piece of the shell. No one was seriously injured.

Lieutenant Chaplin, Master Blue, Midshipman Snell, and Engineer Trilley, with sixty armed men, under the command of Captains Palmer and Woodbury were put ashore. The men scouted the point and returned to the ship at 8 o'clock with two horses captured from Confederate cavalry pickets. They found no battery, only a camp estimated to contain 500 men. The horses were hoisted aboard the *James Guy* and sent to Washington as prizes.

When no battery was found, General Mansfield refused to reconsider his position. A battery on Mathias Point had also become a concern of the civilian population. It was reported in the *New York Tribune* that batteries on Mathias Point would certainly close the Potomac and be impregnable to attack except from behind. Ward, who considered the maintenance of free navigation for Union shipping to be his personal responsibility, informed Captain Dahlgren that he was going to capture Mathias Point himself with the limited resources under his command. In preparation he acquired from the *Pawnee* two boats with armed crews under the command of Lieutenant J. C. Chaplin. The *Pawnee* also supplied Ward with tar, turpentine, oakum, canvas, rope, a lantern, coal bags, and all the shovels, axes, and hatchets on board with the exception of those needed by the cook. The boats and supplies were towed by the *Resolute* down the Potomac from the mouth of Aquia Creek to the area of Mathias Point where Ward was waiting with the *Thomas Freeborn*. Ward's objective was to cut down and burn the brush and trees making activity on Mathias Point visible from the river and to construct and man a Union battery which would prevent the Confederates from gaining control of the point and blockading the Potomac.

On the morning of June 27, 1861, Ward shelled Mathias Point heavily with the guns of the *Thomas Freeborn* to drive the Confederates away. At 10 a.m., he personally led a party ashore. It consisted of thirty-four seamen under the command of Lieutenant Chaplin. He was assisted by Master's Mate John Kellogg of the *Thomas Freeborn*. After a brief encounter with enemy pickets, they set to work. Within minutes they were attacked again by a force of four to five hundred men. Ward ordered the sailors to return to the small boats in which they had landed and lie off the point. He returned to the *Thomas Freeborn* and again shelled the point forcing the rebels to retreat. The sailors then returned to the point and resumed their work.

Burning the brush on the point was slow and difficult because the wood was green and wet. The construction of the sandbag breastwork proceeded quickly; hundreds of the *Pawnee*'s coal bags were filled with dirt and put in place. At about 5 p.m. Commander Ward signalled Chaplin to bring the landing party back to the ship. Most of the tools were returned to the boats. In order to disguise the earthwork which was almost complete, the sailors threw brush over it. It was to be finished the next day and the guns installed. Just as the last of the tools were being gathered up and the landing party was preparing to leave the beach, the Confederates attacked again in greater numbers than before. The dense underbrush allowed the rebels to get within two hundred and fifty yards of the landing party before their presence was known. Most were members of Colonel J. M. Brockenbrough's 40th Virginia Volunteers; others were from Confederate camps in close proximity to Mathias Point.

The sailors quickly returned to their boats as they had during the prior attack. Although the firing was very intense, they were confident that they would be protected by the big guns of the *Thomas Freeborn* as they had before. Only the guns of the *Thomas Freeborn* were silent! The men were left to their fate. Chaplin, who had waited until all the sailors were accounted for before leaving the beach, had to swim to his boat which had drifted from shore, with a wounded sailor on his back. Chaplin received a musket hole in his hat. The flagstaff on his boat was shot away and the flag hit nineteen times. In another boat, the flagstaff was also shot away but a wounded sailor caught the flag and waved it over his head all the way back to the ship. All three boats were riddled with shots. Four sailors were wounded, two of them seriously.

When the boats got alongside the *Thomas Freeborn,* they learned why the ship's guns had not protected their retreat. Ward had been hit in the abdomen by a musket ball fired by a Confederate sharpshooter while he was sighting his forward gun. In the confusion which followed, no one gave orders to fire the ship's guns. Ward died of internal hemorrhage about an hour after being shot. He was the first U. S. Naval Officer of the Civil War to die in action.

Ward had sent the *Resolute* back up the Potomac to assist the *Pawnee* in its duty. He requested that it be sent back twice a day to check on him. Commander Rowan of the *Pawnee,* who

Cdr. James H. Ward, the first U.S. Naval officer of the Civil War to die in action, was killed in an engagement at Mathias Point on June 17, 1861. Only the *Thomas Freeborn* should be pictured and the ship's gun should not be shown firing. *Official and Illustrated War Record*, courtesy Fort Ward Museum.

Reenactment of the death of Cdr. James H. Ward on board the *Thomas Freeborn. The Photographic History of the Civil War.*

was concerned for the safety of Ward and the landing party, immediately dispatched the *Reliance* to Mathias Point in case Ward needed help. The *Reliance* arrived too late to be of much assistance. With the *Pawnee*'s boats in tow, the *Reliance* and *Thomas Freeborn* got under way and rendezvoused with the *Pawnee* near the mouth of Aquia Creek.

The *Pawnee* then proceeded to the Navy Yard with the wounded and Ward's body which was sent ashore at 11 a.m., June 28th with an escort of forty men. Funeral services were held in Washington. His body, accompanied by some of the *Freeborn*'s crew, was then sent to the Brooklyn Navy Yard where another service was held July 1st on board the *North Carolina,* a ship which he had formerly commanded.

The mission, to capture and hold Mathias Point, was a fail-ure—one dead, four wounded, a half-completed breastwork and a gift to the Confederates of shovels, spades, picks, axes, a spy-glass, rope and rifles which had to be abandoned in the retreat.

The Confederates reported no casualties even though it was the first action many of the men had seen. Captain Fleet W. Cox, 40th Virginia, thanked his lucky stars. A cannon ball from the *Freeborn* fell near him but did not explode. Cox had left southern Maryland to join the Confederate Army.

Major Robert M. Mayo, whose regiment rushed to Mathias Point from Brooke Station, was both pleased and frustrated. He told Ruggles he did not realize until the Union landing "how absolutely necessary artillery is at this point. With a single-bored 12-pounder I could have sunk the steamer without expos-ing my men." The Confederate authorities reinforced Mathias Point in case the Federals attempted to land again. Altogether there were about fifteen hundred men stationed there, consist-ing of fifteen companies of volunteers and a section of Walk-er's battery.

In July Confederate authorities decided not to establish a battery there. The force on Mathias Point was deemed insuf-

Funeral services were held for Cdr. James H. Ward in the Brooklyn Navy Yard on board the *North Carolina*, a ship which he commanded prior to his duty with the Potomac Flotilla. *Leslie's Illustrated Weekly.*

ficient to repel a large scale assault and it was too far away from the Confederate main camp to be reinforced. General Lee came to regard Mathias Point as somewhat of a nuisance from then on. He thought, in spite of its commanding position of the Potomac, it would be of "no more importance than other points on the river had troops never been stationed there." But, if he withdrew, the Yankees would surely take it. He, therefore, left the force on the point but ordered the troops to keep out of sight and do nothing to attract the attention of the Potomac Flotilla. He hoped Federal apprehension would be allayed, if he convinced them he had no intention of fortifying Mathias Point.

The *Reliance* was posted off Mathias Point from sunrise to sunset to protect passing vessels. Lieutenant Commanding R. B. Lowry was ordered to assume command of the *Thomas Freeborn.* Commander Thomas T. Craven, on court-martial duty in New York, was directed to Washington on July 9th to take command of the Potomac Flotilla. He selected the U.S.S. *Yankee* as his flagship. The Flotilla by then consisted of the *Pocahontas, Pawnee, Yankee, Freeborn, Release* (also known as *Ice Boat*), *Reliance, Chaplin, Dana, Bailey,* and *Howell Cobb.*

The U.S. Government, in spite of Lee's directive and decision not to fortify Mathias Point, was continually concerned about the point. Rumors reached various authorities in Washington, and anonymous letters and telegrams were sent to President Lincoln and the Secretary of the Navy that batteries were being constructed. Escaped slaves, picked up crossing the Potomac, attested to having been employed constructing earthworks. Some ship captains claimed to have seen men on Mathias Point; others, to having been shot at. Evidence was overwhelmingly indicative that a battery was secretly being built. This elicited the following letter from Gideon Welles, Secretary of the Navy, to Simon Cameron, Secretary of War, on August 20th.

> Sir: The importance of keeping open the navigation of the Potomac is so obvious that no argument is necessary on the subject. So far as possible, this Department has and will continue to discharge its duty in this matter by an

armed flotilla; but there are one or two points
where shore batteries can be made to inter-
cept communications, and in view of that danger and recent investigations, I would most
urgently request that immediate measures be
taken by the War Department to fortify and en-
trench Mathias Point. A single regiment, aided
by two of our steamers, could, heretofore,
and perhaps may still take possession and secure it; but, if more than a regiment is required, it appears to me indispensable that
the requisite number should be furnished. Attention on separate occasions, has been called
to the particular necessity of having that place
as absolutely necessary to the unrestricted
navigation of the Potomac. The Navy will,
at any moment, contribute its efforts toward
seizing and holding that place and apprehend,
there need be no delay. Cannot a sufficient
force be sent down forthwith to seize, and in
connexion [*sic*] with such armed vessels that
we can order, hold Mathias Point and thus
keep the navigation of the Potomac. . . .
Should the insurgents get possession of that
point, it would require a very large force to
dispossess them.

It was hoped that the Army would cooperate. The Navy
was ready to land troops any time they could be sent down
river. They never went. A reconnaissance by General John
Barnard, Chief Engineer of the Army, and Captain Wyman of the
Flotilla, in late September, revealed no fortifications. Rumors
that batteries were being prepared continued to come to the
War Department and Navy Department. The Flotilla watched it
carefully but due to the heavy growth of underbrush it could
not be determined with certainty that no battery existed.
Colonel Charles K. Graham of the Fifth Regiment Excelsior
Brigade (74th N.Y.) stationed near Port Tobacco was as concerned about Mathias Point as the officers of the Flotilla. He
ordered Captain Arthur Wilkinson of his regiment to seize small
boats in the Port Tobacco area, man them with men from the
company and reconnoiter the Potomac shores and Maryland

creeks keeping a close watch on the actions of suspected secession sympathizers. Graham, as a result, became convinced that no batteries existed on Mathias Point. Captain Arnold Harris of the *Island Belle* and Lieutenant Commanding Samuel Magraw of the *Freeborn* at times assisted Graham's men in their reconnaissances. They also came to believe that no batteries existed on Mathias Point. These three men, without the knowledge or approval of General Hooker or the Navy Department, planned a landing on Mathias Point convinced that the odds for a successful reconnaissance were in their favor. At the last minute Magraw with the *Freeborn* could not make it. Acting Master William T. Street of the schooner *Dana* volunteered to replace him.

On the afternoon of November 10th Street went about seizing boats for the embarkation of the troops. Late that night the steamer *Island Belle* with the *Dana* in tow ran up Port Tobacco Creek to Chapel Point and embarked four hundred men of Colonel Graham's regiment. Then they headed for Mathias Point to ascertain positively whether or not batteries existed on the point and put the rumors to rest.

An extensive examination was made under the direction of Harris and Graham for four miles inland. They discovered a few rifle pits, and a partially masked battery in which no guns had been mounted. It had not been used in sometime. They met some Confederate pickets—one was killed, one wounded and the rest fled. Several houses and barns including the Grymes' house, which the rebels had frequently used, were burned. Numerous attempts were made to burn the woods on the point but the timber was too green and wet. The only earthworks on Mathias Point were unmasked to the fire of passing boats.

At 9 a.m. they re-embarked and headed back for Port Tobacco. The expedition was a complete success. No guns or camps were located on the point and the only earthworks were exposed. When informed of the landing and its results, Hooker decided to overlook Graham's indiscretion. "As it appears to have had no unfortunate consequence so far as I have

Old Navy Department Building. *Battles and Leaders.*

learned," Hooker said, "I shall not censure him, but in the future no operation will be projected without my sanction."

Since the security of Mathias Point was considered essential to the free navigation of the Potomac River, the Navy guarded it closely. Welles continued to solicit the cooperation of the War Department in capturing and holding it. In the opinion of the Navy Department only a Union battery on Mathias Point could guarantee it would not be fortified and used by the Confederates to impede Potomac River communications. It remained a constant concern to Federal authorities and within weeks of the November 11th landing rumors concerning Mathias Point began again. To discourage encampments and construction of a battery, it was frequently shelled by a ship of the Flotilla.

U.S. Naval boat practice on the Potomac River. *Official and Illustrated War Record,* courtesy Fort Ward Museum.

Balloon view of Washington, D.C., Spring, 1861. *Harper's Weekly*, July 27, 1861.

CHAPTER VI

ALL IS NOT SO QUIET ON THE POTOMAC

Keeping the Virginia shore free of batteries was only part of the job given to the Potomac Flotilla. In compliance with President Lincoln's blockade of the South, it was to restrict traffic between the Virginia and Maryland shores. When ordered to take over the command of the Flotilla on July 9, 1861, Commander Thomas T. Craven was reminded by Gideon Welles: "It is very important that a full and final end should be put to the intercourse between the two shores, and the capture or destruction of all vessels engaged in the crime is fully warranted."

The residents of southern Maryland were notoriously sympathetic with their neighbors across the river. Information, mail, and supplies, including munitions, were sent from St. Mary's and Charles Counties to Virginia. The Maryland shore abounded in creeks and nooks in which small boats could be secreted by day and run out by night. With citizen cooperation, controlling the traffic would have been a prodigious task; without it, the job was impossible. Acting Master Budd of the U.S.S. *Resolute* reported that according to his observations and calculations there were more supplies accumulated at St. Mary's than its citizens could use in three years. John A. Kennedy, Superintendent of the New York Metropolitan Police Department, in a letter to Secretary of State Seward, cited information he received that pistols, fuses and other arms were being taken from Philadelphia to Virginia by vessels carrying hay. His informants said that the price for the contraband was so good that even ships in the government employ were engaged in the trade.

Commander Ward believed Budd's Ferry was a rebel supply depot. Boats crossed nightly to Quantico Creek often with oarlocks wrapped in sheepskin to keep the noise down. Until a

47

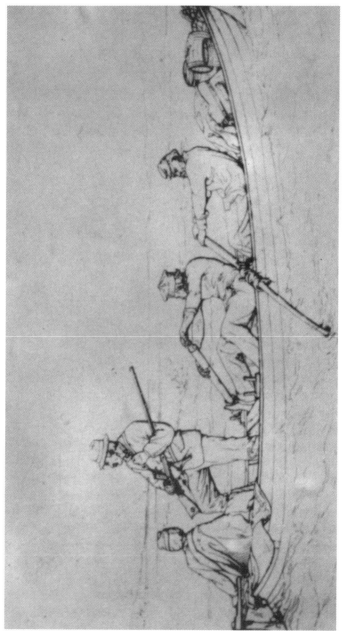

Sketch by Confederate artist Adalbert Volck, showing Marylanders taking men, mail, munitions and other supplies from southern Maryland to Virginia. Note the muffled oarlocks. Courtesy Fort Ward Museum.

schooner was available for duty there, an armed launch was sent to watch for boats. Between passes of the steamers, the sloop *James Skidmore* and other boats ferried goods from Stump Neck to Cockpit Point and Evansport. All individuals who were caught crossing the river were arrested and their boats seized. Some of the vessels were towed to the Navy Yard; others were taken to the Virginia shore and burned. An Admiralty Court determined whether those confiscated should be condemned or released. Some were appropriated for use by the Navy on the Potomac.

The actions of the Flotilla reduced the traffic across the river and made the trip dangerous. Captain F. Cox was prevented from visiting his girl friend in Maryland as a result and complained strongly in his letters. To stop communication completely a boat was needed every hundred yards for miles along the river which was an impossibility. As an alternative, Commander Craven suggested land batteries with two or three regiments on the Maryland points used by the insurrectionists such as Marshall's Point, Indian Head, Stump Neck, Budd's Ferry, Smith's Point, Lower Thom's and Upper Cedar Points, and the mouth of Port Tobacco River. The Army rejected the proposal. Failing that, Craven was directed on August 2nd to "search without further warrant, upon the Maryland shore for arms, ammunition or supplies where there are reasonable grounds for believing they are intended for the rebels." With the aid of Marines frequent raids were made particularly at Leonardtown, Port Tobacco, and Pope's Creek which were considered the principal depots. Even the contents of the Nanjemoy Post Office, in Charles County, were seized and sent to the Dead Letter office in Washington. It was suspected of being a rebel communication center and letters intended for parties in Virginia were often addressed to William S. Brown or George W. Carpenter through the Nanjemoy Post Office.

The raids were rarely successful. News of an impending search always preceded the search party. People such as George Dent regularly thwarted the efforts of the Flotilla. He lived on a high bluff opposite Mathias Point with a good view of the river. He, along with other Marylanders in similar positions, sig-

The U.S.S. *Pawnee* chasing a vessel suspected of smuggling goods from Maryland to Confederate forces in Virginia. *Official and Illustrated War Record*, courtesy Fort Ward Museum.

naled the movements of the Flotilla to the rebels in Virginia with lanterns. Dent was also very actively engaged in transporting mail, passengers and munitions across the river. Mail, sent from Virginia, was frequently addressed in care of George Dent. His men were among the most skillful in crossing the Potomac. To avoid the Flotilla they often hand carried their boats to unguarded areas. In September four of his boats were captured in Pope's Creek; they were some of the best on the river. On November 11th Colonel Charles K. Graham of the 74th New York Infantry, attached to Hooker's Division, finally caught Dent and his son engaged in their favorite pastime. Graham came upon the pair while making his reconnaissance of Mathias Point. They were arrested and sent to Hooker's camp. Dent was armed and carried incriminating papers.

Of all the ships in the Flotilla the one most feared was the *Pawnee*. She was the largest and had the most formidable guns. Lieutenant Hunter H. Lewis, C.S.N., watched a few times as a commercial steamer, the *St. Nicholas*, pulled along side the *Pawnee* and transferred supplies without apparent challenge. The Confederates devised a plan based on these observations to capture the *Pawnee*. With it, they expected to be able to rid the Potomac of the smaller vessels of the Flotilla or, at the very least, open a section of the river, probably between Quantico and Occoquan Creeks, to free trade and communication with Maryland.

There is some dispute as to whether the plan to capture the *Pawnee* was devised by Lieutenant Lewis or Captain George N. Hollins, C.S.N., the principal perpetrator of the capture. The details of the plot were worked out in Richmond where Hollins had gone, with the assistance of Dr. Hooe whose house the Yankees burned in October, to convince authorities of the feasibility of the plan. He won Governor Letcher's approval and was introduced to Colonel Richard Thomas, C.S.A., whose late father had been presiding officer of the Maryland Senate. Thomas was immediately sold on the capture. They returned to Maryland, Thomas with a draft from Richmond for one thousand dollars to purchase arms and ammunitions. At 4 p.m. June 28th, in the disguise of a French lady, he boarded the

St. Nicholas in Baltimore. He assumed the disguise of a woman to remove suspicion from the large trunks he took on board. They were the type a milliner would use but contained the arms and ammunition needed for the capture.

At Point Lookout, Maryland, Captain Hollins boarded in the disguise of an elderly gentleman. Both Thomas and Hollins were accompanied by supporters from Maryland including two of Hollins' sons who were in the guise of ordinary passengers. Everything seemed normal on board the *St. Nicholas.* The music and frivolity signaled the end of another week. A few minutes after the ship pulled away from the dock at Point Lookout, about midnight, Hollins gave a signal, the disguises were shed, arms seized from the trunks and the ship captured. The *St. Nicholas* was then taken to the Coan River Landing in Virginia to await the pre-arranged arrival of Lieutenant Lewis and Colonel Bate's Tennessee regiment who were to assist in capturing the *Pawnee.* The passengers were landed and those who wished were allowed to return to Baltimore. While waiting for Lewis, Hollins occupied himself with a copy of the Baltimore morning paper. From it he ascertained that Commander Ward had been killed and that all of the gunboats were at Washington so the Flotilla's officers and men could attend the funeral services. The well laid plans for the capture of the *Pawnee* were for naught!

Fearful of remaining on the Potomac with an unarmed ship in daylight, Hollins put out to the Chesapeake Bay. Before running up the Rappahannock to the safety of Fredericksburg, Hollins captured three ships. The first was the brig *Monticello* with a load of coffee for Baltimore. Hollins took the brig's crew on board the *St. Nicholas* leaving only the Captain and his wife on the ship with Lieutenant Robert D. Minor. Compensation for the coffee, which was a treat for the "boys in grey" was made at 12¢ a pound to the Baltimore merchants to whom the cargo belonged and sold in Richmond where coffee was scarce for 25 to 30¢ per pound. As the months wore on coffee became even more scarce within Virginia. Eugen O. Perry of the 1st Texas Infantry camped at Dumphries along the Potomac wrote to his brother in November that it cost $1.00 a pound and in

The "French Lady" and Brother Jonathan. This *Harper's Weekly* cartoon mocks the capture of the commercial steamer, *St. Nicholas*, by Confederate forces on the Potomac River. *Harper's Weekly*, July 27, 1861.

December $1.25 per pound. By January the supply had dimin-
ished so that Captain William P. Townsend of the 4th Texas
Regiment complained to his wife that there was but "a scanty
supply of coffee."

The second ship captured, the *Mary Pierce,* was a schooner
from Boston loaded with ice and bound for Washington. It was
sent to Fredericksburg where the hospitals were in desperate
need of ice. The Captain of the vessel attended the sale of the
cargo and was awed by the high price paid for it. As a result he
proposed to Hollins that he return to Boston for another load
and let Hollins capture him a second time with the two men
dividing the profits. "Would anyone but a Yankee have been
guilty of such rascality?" remarked Hollins when he recounted
the story. The *Margaret* with a cargo of coal was captured just
in time to replenish the *St. Nicholas'* supply.

The *St. Nicholas* was bought by the Confederate Government for about $45,000. She was converted into a gunboat
and took several more prizes before being burned at Fredericksburg in 1862. Colonel Thomas, also known by the alias Richard
T. Zarvona, was captured during another ship capturing exploit
and imprisoned, first at Fort McHenry and later at Fort Lafay-
ette in New York Harbor. He was released in a prisoner exchange in 1863. Hollins continued an active career in the Confederate Navy.

Although Hollins and Thomas were convinced that they
would have succeeded in capturing the *Pawnee* if the gunboats
were not in the Navy Yard for Ward's funeral, the odds were
against it. Unknown to them Ward was warned by the Secretary
of the Navy on June 15th that the *St. Nicholas* was suspected of
carrying contraband articles destined for Virginia. Welles ordered
that the ship be stopped and searched. On the 17th of June,
Ward reported that "I have already given the *St. Nicholas* such
an overhauling as will render her circumspect, but on her next
trip will search her thoroughly." Under such circumstances,
the *St. Nicholas* would not have been able to approach the *Pawnee* in a nonchalant manner as if to transfer supplies and then
overwhelm the *Pawnee's* crew and capture her.

Rumors reached Washington of plans to capture other vessels on the Potomac. The *Resolute* narrowly missed being taken in a Maryland inlet. Six hundred Virginia riflemen with two field pieces crossed the river and were waiting for the ship. They arrived too late, however. Acting Master Budd got wind of the plan and dropped down the river during the night.

When attempts to capture the *Pawnee* and other ships failed, the Confederates tried another approach. They conceived a plan to destroy ships on the Potomac. On July 7th, two weeks before the First Battle of Manassas, two torpedoes were planted in the river off Aquia Creek. The *Pawnee* went within two hundred yards of them. They were spotted and boats were sent out from the *Resolute,* which was nearby, to snag them. One was sunk in the process.

Civil War torpedoes, it must be remembered, were really mines. They were not self-propelled and generally fell into one of three categories: those detonated by contact with a ship, those exploded by an electric current from shore, and those set off by means of a burning fuse. The one which was not sunk belonged to the third category and was sent to Captain Dahlgren at the Navy Yard for a thorough examination. Mr. Budd of the *Resolute* has left a sketch and a description based on his preliminary examination. The "wicked devise" as Commander Rowan of the *Pawnee* called it, consisted of two watertight eighty gallon oil casks which were used as buoys. They were connected by twenty-five fathoms of three and one-half inch rope buoyed with large squares of cork every two feet, secured to the casks by iron handles. Suspended from the casks, six feet under water, was a bomb of boiler iron heavily riveted, fitted with a brass tap and filled with powder. On top of the cask was a wooden box with a fuse in a gutta-percha tube. The greater length of the fuse was coiled in a cork in the middle of the cask. Luck, again, seemed to be riding the waves with the Flotilla.

The *Freeborn*, it would appear, needed luck just to remain afloat. Perhaps the Confederates knew of its condition for they never attempted to capture or destroy her. Given time the *Free-*

Two torpedoes were placed in the Potomac River off Aquia Creek by the Confederate forces in an effort to destroy the U.S.S. *Pawnee*. They were discovered before the *Pawnee* ran into them. *Frank Leslie's American Soldier.*

born might have sunk or had a gun explode. Lieutenant R. B. Lowry, the Captain, complained on July 10th that the 32-pounder was "vent-worn, cracked and unsafe," the gun carriages were broken from over-use, the engines in need of repair, the ammunition low, the crews exhausted. And if that were not enough cause for concern, he reported that the ship also leaked badly. The engagements at Aquia Creek and Mathias Point had taken a heavy toll on the *Freeborn*. She was repaired after the Aquia exchange but really needed a complete overhaul to be put back in good condition. The converted ferry was made serviceable but not the fighting ship Ward had known.

Many other ships of the Flotilla, for that matter, were in need of repairs but most could not be spared from duty long enough to do the required work. Stop gap measures were used until the condition became critical. The U.S.S. *Union,* for example, took so much water that bailing became a full-time job for her crew. When bailing became futile Lieutenant A. Harrell was ordered to take her to the Philadelphia Navy Yard for repairs. It took only a cursory examination for the yardmen to decide the *Union* was a hopeless case. She was de-commissioned on December 10, 1861.

On July 21st the Confederate Army defeated the Union force at the First Battle of Manassas. Most of General Holmes' Brigade left Aquia to provide reserve support and they returned to their camps after the battle. General Johnston moved up to Fairfax Court House with outposts as close to Washington as Munson's Hill.

Come August the Federal authorities were faced with a new problem on the Potomac. Frequent reports were received by the War Department from so-called "indisputable authorities" that the rebels were gathering a flotilla of their own consisting of the recently armed *George Page,* scows and flatboats anchored up Aquia Creek. It was felt this was indicative of an impending invasion of Maryland and perhaps even an attempt to capture Washington. The Navy confirmed the presence of the boats and discovered new earthworks at the mouth of Aquia Creek. Major General George B. McClellan, Commanding the Army of the

Potomac, under General Scott who was still General-in-Chief, addressed Secretary Welles:

> I have, today, received additional information which convinces me that the enemy will, within a very short time, attempt to throw a respectable force from the mouth of Aquia Creek into Maryland. This attempt will probably be preceded by the erection of batteries at Mathias and White House Points. Such a movement on the part of the enemy, in conjunction with others probably designed, would place Washington in great jeopardy. I most urgently urge that the strongest possible naval force be at once concentrated at the mouth of Aquia Creek and that a vigilant watch be maintained so as to render such a passage of the river absolutely impossible.

The following day a statement, attributed to Jefferson Davis, was received by the Navy Department. Its source, although unidentified, was regarded as absolutely credible. The note was directed to the pro-Southerners in Maryland. It said, "Have no street fights; keep Baltimore quiet for the present; in ten days I shall command the Potomac and cross between Mathias Point and Aquia Creek into Charles and St. Mary's Counties (they are all friends there) and march upon Annapolis. Then, having the two approaches to Washington in possession, let Baltimore rise and burn the bridges. The movements in the upper Potomac are only feints."

Maryland's Governor, Thomas H. Hicks, was certain that just such a movement was in the works. Once Maryland's commitment was made to the Union, he wanted no part of riots or invasions in support of the South. He begged the Secretary of War to provide an army and naval force strong enough to repel the expected movement. He concluded by saying, "Do not think me scared; I only wish to head off the rebels." Most of the Flotilla including the *Yankee, Pocahontas, Ice Boat, Reliance, Mount Vernon, Freeborn, Resolute* and *Pawnee* were gathered off Aquia Creek in response to the threat. Orders were issued by

Gideon Welles to Commander Craven to destroy all boats on the Maryland and Virginia shore if an invasion of Maryland appeared imminent.

The expected invasion never materialized. The Confederates were not in a position to undertake anything that might result in a major confrontation at that time. It was coincidental that they were collecting boats on the Virginia side at the same time the rumors were arriving in Washington. Union estimates of Confederate strength were then, and continued for some time, to be unreliable and exaggerated.

Probably because of their anxiety for action, the officers and men in the Confederate camps along the Potomac also expected to invade Maryland. Captain Fleet Cox wrote his "Miss Mollie" that he looked forward to seeing fifty thousand Virginia and Georgia volunteers on the soil of Maryland "to prove to the Yankees that Maryland is part of the sunny South and shall be free." With a little vanity he told her he hoped she would be able to see him drill his Potomac Rifles in Port Tobacco after they crossed the river.

Communication between the Maryland and Virginia shores was a problem. An effort was made by the Flotilla to search every vessel suspected of engaging in illicit trade. Launches sent out from the ships rounded up all the small boats they could find on the Virginia shore and many of those in the Maryland creeks. In mid-August William Budd of the *Resolute* saw a boat on the Virginia shore near Persimmon Point just below Mathias Point. He dispatched a boat to get it. Just as they were preparing to fasten the boat to theirs they were ambushed from the shore. Three of the boat's crew were killed and one wounded.

Buildings along the Virginia shore were also carefully watched to see that they were not being used as depots for goods ferried across the Potomac. A collection of houses below Freestone Point became suspect when rebel pickets and three camp wagons were seen near them. A ship of the Flotilla shelled the nearby area to clear it of troops and sent a landing party

A boat was sent out from the *Resolute* to capture a scow which was stuck in the mud near Persimmon Point on the Virginia shore of the Potomac. It appeared to contain barrels of powder. Just as the bowsman was preparing to capture the scow, the boat's crew was ambushed from shore by Confederate soldiers. *Illustrated London News*, courtesy Frederick Hicks.

ashore to check out the buildings. When they were found to contain a considerable supply of stores, they were burned to the ground.

One of the Navy's most daring exploits occurred on October 11, 1861. The rebels had been fitting out a large schooner, the *Martha Washington,* in Quantico Creek. With a sizable number of troops in the immediate area, it was presumed by the U.S. Navy that the vessel would ultimately be used to ferry rebel soldiers across the Potomac. Lieutenant Commanding Abram D. Harrell with his gig and two other launches entered the mouth of Quantico Creek as quietly as possible at 2:30 a.m. on October 11th. The men, who were within pistol range of either shore searched for the schooner in the darkness. They found her tied up close to shore with one sentry posted. He immediately fled to alarm the camps. The sailors boarded the schooner, piled the cabin furniture and watched as Acting Master Amos P. Foster of the *Resolute* applied the torch that doomed the ship.

That they made it back to the Potomac is another one of those believe it or not happenings on the Potomac during the war. The flames from the burning schooner guided them back to the Potomac but also marked their position for the rebel soldiers on the shores. Not a man was killed but their clothes and the boats were perforated with holes. For his gallant achievement Harrell received a commendation and the promise of a better command from Gideon Welles, Secretary of the Navy.

The Flotilla's efforts at reducing inter-shore communications were only partially successful. Traffic continued throughout the war and those engaged in it became very skillful, vigilant, and elusive.

On October 11, 1861, a detachment from the Potomac Flotilla entered Quantico Creek and burned the Confederate schooner, *Martha Washington. Frank Leslie's Illustrated Newspaper.*

CHAPTER VII

THE POTOMAC IS CLOSED

What the Confederates really had in mind was not an invasion of Maryland, but the establishment of land batteries on the Virginia bank effective enough to stop the Union from using the Potomac. With a section of the river fortified it was hoped that a free trade area of the river could be established. The battery at Aquia was incapable of closing the Potomac. Mathias Point, although strategically located, was too far from the Confederate main force to be supported if it were attacked. There were numerous other promontories on the Potomac that would better serve the purpose. As one travels from Washington to Aquia on the river, there is White House or White Stone Point, Hallowing Point, High Point, Freestone Point, Cockpit Point, Possum Nose, Possum Point, Shipping Point and Evansport. If one compares the "McDowell Map" which was based on a geological survey with maps of today, a difference will be noted in the location of Possum Nose. Today's maps show it to be very close to, almost connected to Cockpit Point. During the Civil War period there was uncertainty as to its exact location but it was placed farther down the river, generally around Possum Point. In 1861 and 1862 Possum Nose of today and Cockpit Point were regarded as one point, Cockpit Point.

Although the river for miles above the mouth of the Occoquan is narrower than anywhere below, the Confederates could not establish and hope to maintain batteries so near to Alexandria because of the close proximity of the Union army. Below the Occoquan there is a section not as narrow but still adaptable to a close blockade. This would include Freestone Point at the mouth of Neabsco Creek to Evansport, one-half mile below the mouth of Quantico Creek. To this area the Confederates turned their attention.

63

As early as June 4th Captain Lynch and General Ruggles recommended that a battery be built at Evansport. The projecting shore was a mile long which would enable gunners to keep ships under constant fire for a long time. Also, the Maryland shore across the river was suitable for ferry landings and had roads leading to the interior which would come in handy if a decision to cross the river were made. A battery at Mathias Point had not been ruled out when General Holmes expressed his preference for Evansport in a letter to Colonel George Deas, Assistant Adjutant General of the Confederate Army, written on June 27th:

> If it be the wish of the commanding general that a battery should be erected to prevent free navigation of the Potomac River, I would respectfully recommend that the neighborhood of Evansport should be preferred to Mathias Point. There is little difference in the distance of the channel from the shore, and large guns will command either. From Evansport there is a good road to Fredericksburg and a good road to Manassas, whereas from Mathias Point it would require a long land travel to any vulnerable point. If you can send me two 32-pounders or two 8-inch columbiads, I believe I can stop the navigation of the river.

General Lee was impressed with Holmes' views but hesitated to give his whole-hearted approval until another examination was made. This was to be carried out by naval officers under Holmes' direction. They were cautioned not to make any unnecessary demonstrations which might attract attention and disclose their purposes. Lee even promised the three 9-inch columbiads originally intended for Mathias Point if Evansport proved to be a more satisfactory location.

Commander C. H. Kennedy, C.S.N., made the reconnaissance. He found the distance from shore to shore to be 2,513 yards. He also observed that there were two channels with a middle area between them. The main channel ran on the Virginia side; the other, narrow and winding, ran along the Maryland shore. People familiar with the river told him that ships drawing more than twelve feet of water could not use the narrow channel. With 9-inch guns and one rifled 12-pounder Kennedy was certain the river could be closed during the day. At night tugs and smaller boats could steal by on the Maryland shore protected by the darkness.

On the basis of this report and the opinion of General Holmes, Evansport was selected over Mathias Point. On August 22, 1861, Holmes received orders: "You will now cause to be erected with as little delay as possible the battery at Evansport." General Joseph Johnston was instructed to furnish a competent engineering officer to superintend its construction and command the troops stationed there. General Isaac R. Trimble from his adopted Maryland was the man selected for the job on September 3rd. Like Aquia Creek it was to be a joint army-navy project and Commander Frederick Chatard, C.S.N., was the actual commander of the battery. Work was begun and not one but several batteries were constructed. The first was ready for service on September 29th; another on October 9th. On the 21st Lieutenant R.D. Minor, C.S.N., was sent from Richmond to fit sights to the 42 and 32-pounder guns. Most of the work was done at night behind a shield of trees. In spite of being on the river's edge, they were so cautious their activity went undetected by the U.S. Navy. Holmes, Trimble and Chatard were ready for action. They felt confident that they could close the river and repel any attempt to capture the batteries with the troops at Evansport supported by General W. H. C. Whiting's Brigade. Whiting, an extremely competent engineer, who graduated first in his class from West Point, was responsible for the defense of the Occoquan-Potomac front. His Brigade was camped in the Dumphries area and was to come to the aid of the batteries along the river if a Union landing were attempted.

The sound of the guns at Evansport was not immediately heard. General Joe Johnston requested that they not be fired until he made some arrangements of his own. What those arrangements were could not be determined. More batteries were constructed during this period of ordered silence. About twenty guns were put in place. Some of them, 10-pound Parrotts, 12-pound Parrotts, and a 30-pound Parrott were captured from the Yankees at Manassas. They also had at least three 32-pounders, an unknown number of 42-pounders and the Tredgar Works in Richmond which produced heavy cannons was instructed to send a rifle columbiad. Another gun, an English Blakely of long range, had been run through the blockade via Bermuda. There is some question as to whether the gun was an Armstrong or English Blakely. It is referred to by both names. It is possible that those using it did not know which they had.

Unfortunately, no detailed Confederate maps or descriptions of the batteries have been found, so it is impossible to say exactly how many were finally constructed or how many guns were mounted. Official Confederate reports are inadequate. One explanation for the absence of detailed information in private Confederate correspondence might be found in the story that circulated in October, 1861, concerning Dr. Erskine, Surgeon General of the Tennessee Legion. One of his letters described the construction of batteries at Evansport and it appeared in a Memphis newspaper. As a result he was arrested and tried for the indiscretion because Confederate authorities felt he might have jeopardized their position along the Potomac. After hearing the story Captain Nathaniel Dawson of the Fourth Alabama Regiment warned his girl friend to keep his letters private. He was also careful not to reveal anything of military importance which could be put to use by the Yankees if his letters were intercepted or printed. Because of these factors most of the source material is Union sketches and reports which are based on conjecture and observations such as the "McDowell Map" of Northeastern Virginia, Robert S. Williamson's *Survey of Budd's Ferry and Vicinity* and the map drawn by Colonel William F. Small from a balloon on the Maryland shore.

Prior to the establishment of their permanent batteries, the Confederates made use of field batteries both to harass the

The Tredegar Works in Richmond, Virginia. *The Photographic History of the Civil War.*

Flotilla and draw its attention away from the Evansport area. Marlborough Point was an example. They had an encampment of soldiers and five heavy guns on the point at the end of July. The *Yankee* and *Reliance* went in to feel them out. Shots were exchanged. The ships retreated; their guns did not have the range that the Confederate guns possessed. Other exchanges occurred on August 5th and 23rd. On the latter date the *Yankee* and *Release* engaged some field pieces of the Thirtieth Virginia Infantry for about forty minutes. Captain R. L. Walker was in charge of the rebel pieces which consisted of a siege rifled gun and a section (rifle) of Walker's battery. Neither side suffered damages. Marlborough Point, like Aquia, was an annoyance but not a real threat as it did not command the channel.

There were plenty of rumors circulating that other batteries, more formidable, were under construction. A Negro, picked up attempting to cross the Potomac on August 22nd, told Mr. Budd of the *Resolute* that he was being sent to Virginia by Misters Posey and Renner, to help build a battery. (Both Posey and Renner were residents of Maryland.) On September 2nd a young man picked up crossing from Virginia to Maryland said that a fort of some kind was being prepared on Shipping Point, at the mouth of Quantico Creek, and that straw had been laid on the road to facilitate bringing guns from Dumfries.

Commander Craven realized the maintenance of free navigation was rapidly deteriorating. The *Richmond Examiner,* which he believed often contained much truth, ran an article September 9th stating that the Potomac would be closed before too many hours by powerful batteries, ten of which were ready for immediate use. He was apprised by the Navy Department that it was aware of the situation but could do nothing more without the cooperation of the Army. Craven was told to stock up on coal and provisions in case he was cut off from Washington and to choose some place in Maryland for the delivery of supplies by land, if it should become necessary. In Washington the *Daily National Intelligencer* warned its readers that their military authorities were not taking the threats of the Richmond papers seriously enough.

On September 23rd, Lieutenant C.S. Norton, Commanding the U.S.S. *Seminole,* picked up a party of slaves escaping from Virginia. They told of two hundred men with two siege guns passing through their master's place the day before on their way to Freestone Point. After a dawn reconnaissance which assured him that indeed a battery was being built the *Jacob Bell,* under Lieutenant Edward McCrea, moved in on the battery at 9:30 a.m., September 25th and fired six shells dispersing the workmen but drawing no response. The *Seminole,* which had accompanied the *Jacob Bell,* opened fire and was immediately answered, affirming the existence of the battery. Neither ship was damaged but the *Valley City,* a steamer belonging to the Flotilla, received a shot through its bow as it was passing up the river. The *Seminole* towed her to the safety of Indian Head across the river and in the confusion they collided. There appeared to be four guns, one rifled and of extreme range, probably a 30-pounder. They fired on all ships going up or down the river until 3 p.m. The battery was commanded by Colonel Louis T. Wigfall of the First Texas Infantry. In spite of his pension for hard cider Colonel Wigfall, who soon became General Wigfall, of the Texas Brigade, was elected to the Confederate Senate. When he resigned his commission, command of the Brigade was exercised for a short time by a Marylander, Colonel James J. Archer, Fifth Texas Regiment. Colonel John B. Hood replaced him. When Freestone Point was attacked, the North Carolina Sixth was immediately sent to support the troops there in case the Union attempted to land. They camped behind the point for the night and returned to their camp the next day.

Commander Harrell of the *Freeborn* questioned the prudence of letting vessels carrying government stores pass Freestone Point. Although it fired daily on ships that passed, it, like Aquia and Marlborough Point, could not command the channel. Federal authorities concluded since the battery commanded nothing, and the workmen, instead of being concealed, were exposed to view, that it was merely a ruse to draw attention away from more important points until batteries were prepared and the ships could safely pass.

United States Steamer *Jacob Bell.* (O. R. Navies.)

Commander Craven felt he could no longer be responsible for maintaining free navigation on the Potomac with the policy being pursued. "The more I witness the operation of the rebels," he wrote Secretary Welles, "the more I am satisfied that if some prompt and efficient step is not taken to prevent it, the navigation of the Potomac will be entirely cut off." His reference to prompt and efficient action by implication meant an assault on the Virginia shore by the Army with Navy support. Past requests for assistance to secure the river had been denied. The best cooperation he could get after Freestone was another reconnaissance of the Potomac as far as Mathias Point. This one was undertaken by Brigadier General John G. Barnard, Chief Engineer of the Army of the Potomac with the assistance of Captain Wyman of the Potomac Flotilla. They selected the points which were potentially good sites for Confederate batteries. Two were fairly close together, Shipping Point, at the mouth of Quantico Creek, and Evansport between Chopawamsic and Quantico Creeks. The third was Cockpit Point almost midway between Freestone Point and Shipping Point. They regarded Shipping Point as most favorable for a battery with a few drawbacks such as being level, open, no more than twenty to thirty feet high and within range of some of the Flotilla's guns. Evansport, forming the end of the peninsula, was a fairly clear plateau with rising wooded hills in the rear. Unknown to the Union observers, the Confederates had a battery two days away from completion at Evansport. Cockpit Point, wooded, with irregular hills offered numerous places where batteries could be erected to bear a cross fire on the river. A battery was known to exist at Freestone Point; the ones at Aquia Creek and Marlborough Point were regarded as defensive. Mathias Point was not fortified but the thought of its being so caused Navy men to shudder. Barnard communicated his thoughts based on the reconnaissance to General McClellan on September 28th:

> Batteries at High Point and Cockpit Point and thence down to Chopawamsic *cannot* be prevented. We may, indeed, prevent their construction on *certain* points, but along here, somewhere, the enemy can establish, in spite

of us, as many batteries as he chooses. What is the remedy? Favorable circumstances, not to be anticipated nor made the basis of any calculations, might justify and render success- ful the attack of a particular battery. To sup- pose that we can capture them *all,* or by more attacks of this kind prevent the navigation from being molested, is very much the *same* as to suppose that the hostile army in our own front can prevent us building and maintaining field-works to protect Arlington and Alexan- dria, by capturing them one and all as fast as they are built. As long as the enemy is master of the other shore he can build and maintain as many batteries as he chooses.

This was hardly what Craven wanted to hear. The Flotilla could not keep the river open by itself. Since Barnard con- sidered counter-battering the Virginia shore premature and would not go so far as to suggest a military effort to dis- lodge the rebels, General McClellan would hardly initiate one. Nevertheless, Craven and Welles felt they could not wait com- placently while the Confederates further entrenched themselves. Since the Army would not initiate a joint action on the Potomac, the Navy requested one for the third time.

In June and August the Army was asked to cooperate in taking Mathias Point. Both requests were denied. In early Oc- tober the Navy Department proposed to President Lincoln and the War Department that the rebel batteries which had begun to appear on the river be destroyed and their places occupied by the Army. It was a most urgent, you might even say last hope, appeal. The three most heavily armed ships in the Potomac Flotilla, the *Pawnee, Pocahontas,* and *Seminole,* plus the *F. 'B. Forbes,* which had two large guns, were to be detached on October 12th and sent with Commodore Samuel F. Dupont's expedition to Port Royal. They were all powerful, of light draft and had covered machinery. The *Valley City* and *Rescue* were to be detached two weeks later. Ships were very scarce and they were better fitted for the Port Royal expedition than any other vessels the Navy possessed. If anything was to be done to secure the uninterrupted navigation of the Potomac River, it had to be done before the bigger ships left.

President Lincoln liked the idea; a blockaded Washington, D.C., would be a humiliation especially after suffering defeat at Manassas. He, with Gideon Welles and the Assistant Secretary of the Navy, Gustavus V. Fox, urged General McClellan to co-operate. To their surprise, he agreed to send four thousand men down the Potomac to land just above Mathias Point under the protection of the gunboats. The outcome was recalled for the Joint Committee on the Conduct of the War by Gustavus Fox:

> They agreed to send down four thousand men to take possession just above Mathias Point. The orders were sent down from the Navy Department to Commander Craven and Captain Dahlgren; and scows and steamers were provided for carrying the troops and landing them. Captain Craven collected at Mathias Point all the boats of his flotilla, and we notified him that the four thousand men would arrive there in the middle of the night. These troops did not go. The first information that we had of that was a tug sent up the following day from Captain Craven with word that the troops had not come. I went over to see the President about it, and we went over to see General McClellan. He told us that the engineers were of the opinion that the troops could not be landed in such large numbers, and that they had concluded not to send them. I told him that the business of landing troops belonged to the Navy, and that no one had inquired of us whether we could land them or not. It was then concluded that they should go the next night. But the next night they did not go. They never went.

Craven was mortified and furious! If the river were closed, it would be his reputation that would suffer and he was powerless to do any more than he had already done. The

United States Steamer *Pocahontas*. (O. R. Navies.)

Navy Department felt it had done all in its power and could do no more. As for President Lincoln, Fox claimed that "he manifested more feeling and disappointment than I have ever seen him exhibit when he found the men had not gone."

Why did McClellan change his mind? As was his habit, he never fully explained. From conversations with various gentlemen of the War Department, Fox concluded that they were dubious of the ability of the Navy to protect the soldiers on the river bank from attack in their rear. They thought the best way to take the batteries was to march down the river from Alexandria with a strong contingent and drive the Confederates back from the Potomac. Since doing that might have triggered a general engagement, which the War Department, namely General McClellan, wished to avoid, the action was not authorized. But then the question arises, would McClellan ever be ready to initiate a major battle? At that time General Scott was still General-in-Chief of the Army but McClellan had so successfully asserted himself on the Washington scene that he had eroded Scott's authority. Soldier and politician alike deferred to McClellan. He had managed to convince many in official Washington that the old General was responsible for the inaction of the army. Unable to endure McClellan's arrogance any longer, Scott resigned in November. McClellan replaced him.

On October 12th the better part of the Potomac Flotilla was detailed to DuPont's South Atlantic Blockading Squadron. And the Navy Department reconciled itself to the certainty that the Potomac would soon be closed! Reading the Washington newspapers of the day would give one the impression that a blockade was such a horrible thing to contemplate that the very possibility of one should be erased from people's minds. Having reminded the government of its duty to keep the Potomac open, they undertook to prove to their readers that the rumors of its being blockaded were strictly rumors. While admitting the existence of batteries, they discounted them as no more serious to Washington than a splinter in a man's hand. On September 30th, under the caption, "Local Matters," the *Daily National Intelligencer* wrote:

Blocking Up The Potomac—We have daily
reports in regard to the effort of the rebels to
impede the navigation of the Potomac. Some
of these rumors may be by parties interested
in putting up the price of freight or of articles
of necessity usually transported on the Potomac, but the fact stands out prominently that
not a single vessel has yet been prevented from
coming up or going down to its destination.

The article concluded with a list, by name and type of the
vessels docked at Washington or Georgetown. As if to reassure
themselves, the *Daily National Intelligencer* and *Washington Star*
often reported that the number of ships on the river was unprecedented. The *New York Daily Tribune* even got in on the action with an article on October 11th entitled "No Obstruction
to Navigation." It said, "Recent investigations show that there
are not and never have been rebel fortifications on the Potomac
at any other place than Aquia Creek. . . . The guns at Freestone
Point, which a fortnight since fired upon our vessels causing a
fear that navigation might be impeded, was a field battery on
its way south."

Back on the Potomac all indications were that heavy batteries would soon be revealed. Lieutenant E. A. Sherburne, a
deserter from an Arkansas Regiment, was picked up on the Maryland side by Lieutenant McCrea of the *Jacob Bell.* He claimed
that his regiment was camped behind Evansport and that heavy
batteries were being built there and along the connecting shore
for a mile and a half. He mentioned that Lieutenant Simms,
formerly of the U.S. Navy, was one of the officers responsible.
He said four rifled guns and one 64-pounder were in place at
Evansport. Supporting the batteries, there were 10,000 troops
within an hour to an hour and a half radius. McCrea made a
reconnaissance of the shore near Evansport. He could see no
guns but some changes in the land features were evident. There
were also reports of guns on Shipping Point.

The troops in the Dumphries area who would come to the
support of the batteries were those of Whiting's Brigade who were

also guarding the line of the Occoquan against a Union attack. After the retirement of the Confederate Army to the Rappahannock, Whiting wrote a report to the Secretary of War, J. P. Benjamin through General Holmes describing the disposition of troops under his command.

> The disposition of my division was as follows: Hampton's brigade in advance, consisting of four regiments and three batteries. Of this, two regiments and two batteries were at Wolf Run Shoals and Davis Ford, on the Occoquan; the Legion, with one battery, at Colchester, and one regiment near the village of Occoquan, at the forks of the Telegraph and Brentsville roads. This line was ten miles in extent. In support the Texas brigade, Colonel Archer; three regiments of this were posted on the Telegraph road, between and upon Neabsco and Powell's Runs, with one battery. The First Texas at Talbot's Hill, on the Quantico, to cover the left of the Evansport battery. In support the Third Brigade: Fifth Alabama battalion and one company of the First Tennessee at Cockpit battery; one regiment and one battery at Dumphries; and four regiments and one battery on Powell's Run, 3 miles above Dumphries, equidistant from Evansport, Wolf Run Shoals, and Colchester. One squadron of cavalry and the legion of cavalry picketed the Potomac from Evansport to Colchester and the Occoquan in front.

The Confederates intended to reveal all of their batteries at one time. To this end they had been very discreet building them and left a screen of trees cut halfway through in front of each one. When the proper time came they could be felled with the single blow of an ax. The U.S. Navy forced the batteries to show themselves before the Confederates intended to do so. Although they had been detailed to the expedition to attack Port Royal Inlet, South Carolina, the ships did not begin to leave until October 15th. Early in the morning on the 15th Commander Percival Drayton, Captain of the *Pocahontas,* had breakfast with John Dahlgren at his quarters in the Washington Navy Yard. As Drayton was leaving the house Dahlgren jokingly said, "Take care, Drayton, of those batteries." Drayton replied, "I would make them show themselves if I had the authority." After a moment's pause Dahlgren said: "Very well, I will give you authority: have them out."

The most likely place for a hidden battery was, of course, Evansport. At 10:30 a.m. when the *Pocahontas* was abreast, Drayton opened up on the point with three 12-pound rifled shots, two 32-pound shots, one 32-pound shell, and one shell from the pivot gun. Thinking that the batteries had been discovered and were under attack, the trees concealing them were ordered cut down. The Confederates were then ready for action. The *Pocahontas* had by then passed the point and ceased firing. Following close behind her, however, was the *Seminole.* The Evansport batteries were ready and waiting. They fired upon the *Seminole* the entire time she was within range. The *Seminole* returned the fire. The experience was related by Commander Gillis in an informal letter to Commander Craven written the next day:

> Dear Craven:
> Did you hear the row? We had quite a sharp action with the rebel batteries, three in number, as we passed Evansport yesterday. It continued for forty minutes, as the "old wagon" moved leisurely down the river. Two of the forts are on the bank of the river, the other lies inland 300 or 400 yards. They poured the rifle shot and shell into us in a lively manner, which we answered briskly so long as our guns could be brought to bear. We kept steadily on our course, deeming it a matter of more importance to take the vessel uninjured to her destination for work of more consequence than shelling the batteries on the Potomac.

The *Seminole* and *Pocahontas* engaged the Confederate batteries at Evansport on October 15, 1861. Since the picture is printed backwards, the ships appear to be going up the Potomac when they are actually going down the river. *Harper's Weekly*, November 2, 1861.

The *Pocahontas* stirred up the party with a
gun or two as she steamed down ahead of us,
which the batteries did not reply to. She continued on, leaving us to do battle with the
Dixie boys. They did us some damage. The
"varmints" shot away our mizzenmast and
mizzen after shroud, also both mainstays
near masthead, sent two shots through our rail
and hammock nettings, and doing us some injury inboard, as they passed through both sides.
A shell or two burst close under our starboard bow, giving us a fine shower at pivot
guns, and burying some fragments in outside
planking, etc. Our shell fell in around their
works and I think with effect, but of course
they will not acknowledge any damage. . . .
Well, what of it? There was nobody hurt.

Sincerely yours,
Jno. P. G. (illis)

In the wee hours of the morning, October 16th, the *Pawnee*,
accompanied by two tugs, went down the river. The *Mount
Vernon*, loaded with marines, preceded them and passed the
batteries in the dark. By the time the *Pawnee* was opposite
Quantico Creek, the dawn was breaking. Batteries at Shipping
Point and Evansport opened with a hail of fire. Captain R.H.
Wyman, commanding the *Pawnee* in place of Rowan, had decided not to fire upon the batteries unless they were destructive.
Once the guns were readied, the crew was sent to the opposite
side of the deck behind a makeshift barricade. Had the men
been at their stations several of the Number 2 gun's crew would
have been killed. The *Pawnee* was hit six times but not seriously.

On the evening of the 17th three tugs and one steamer were
sent to try the batteries. Two of the tugs passed unobserved;
one was disabled before reaching Shipping Point, and the
steamer refused to attempt passage. The two tugs returned
with commercial vessels in tow. They were shot at but not
hit.

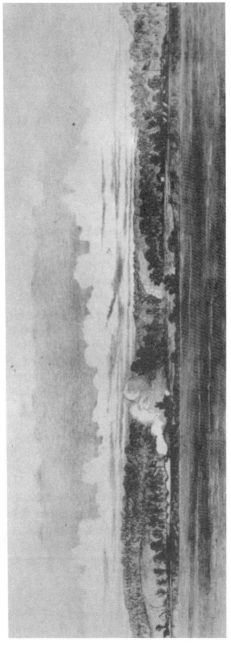

The Confederate Army and Navy jointly built heavy batteries at Evansport and Shipping Point. *Official and Illustrated War Record*, courtesy Fort Ward Museum.

Evansport and Shipping Point were so close together and became so extensively fortified that it soon became difficult to distinguish where the Shipping Point batteries ended and the ones at Evansport began. Guns were also mounted at the mouth of Chopawamsic Creek. In Confederate correspondence all of these batteries are generally referred to as the Evansport batteries.

On the 18th Acting Master Foster of the steamer *E.B. Hale* reported seeing the rebels clear away trees revealing guns on Cockpit Point at 5:30 p.m. It would be a while before Cockpit Point reached full strength. General Trimble suggested a strong battery there to General Johnston on November 16th to extend the Confederate command of the river. Lewis McKenzie, the Union Mayor of Alexandria, who was familiar with it described his impression of Cockpit Point to Secretary Welles on October 26th:

> Cockpit Point where the Confederates have a battery is in some respects a remarkable military position. It commands Freestone Point on the north, Shipping Point on the south, being a distant from either about 2½ miles. The land is higher than either of them and it projects farther into the Potomac. In the rear it is defended by Powell's Creek, the low grounds of which are commanded by it.
> Opposite in Maryland are Stump Neck and Budd's Ferry. The height of the land at Cockpit above the river is from forty to fifty feet, while that of Stump Neck is not more than eight or ten for a distance of one and one half miles back from the river. The river here being 1¼ miles wide, the distance from this rebel battery to high ground in the rear of Stump Neck would be 2¾ miles; to the heights at Budd's Ferry not more than 2½ miles at the most.

This, of course, is a description of Possum Nose and Cockpit as one, not two points. Cockpit Point, which protrudes farther into the river is much lower than Possum Nose and quite

Cockpit Point Battery as seen from the Potomac River. Sketched by A. Lumley. (Note: The location on today's map is Possum Nose next to Cockpit Point.) *Official and Illustrated War Record*, courtesy Fort Ward Museum.

marshy. The rear of Cockpit Point is marked by irregular hills. Possum Nose is a 75 foot hill, not 40 or 50 as thought by McKenzie, with a cliff-like bank fronting the Potomac. A heavy concentration of guns was located on Possum Nose when the Confederate Cockpit Point was brought to full strength.

Captain Bushrod W. Frobel, an artillery officer, who commanded the batteries there incurred the wrath of a local citizen in mid-December. Mr. C.W.C. Dunnington, father of seven children, owned a house with a number of outbuildings on the Potomac two miles from Cockpit Point. Because of its close proximity to the river Dunnington's tenant left the property in October and it was unoccupied in the interval. On the 16th of December when he went to inspect it he found chimneys standing where once there were buildings and his main house a complete wreck. He traced some of the wood to Cockpit Point where he found Captain Frobel erecting winter quarters out of his houses. This was too much even for a loyal Southerner. He denounced the Captain and the State of Virginia, to which he had paid taxes, for failing to protect him. "The country around here is treated more like an enemy country" he declared, "than the homes of loyal citizens. . . . We have no courts of justice or I would prosecute the ruffians."

On December 15th a smaller battery of two pieces was revealed between Cockpit and Shipping Points. It was built by details from the 4th Texas and 18th Georgia Regiments. The battery at Freestone Point appears to have been abandoned after the stronger ones were functional. The principal batteries were located at Evansport (including the guns at the mouth of the Chopawamsic), Shipping Point, and Cockpit Point (Cockpit meaning Possum Nose) and for a time on Freestone Point. This covered a distance of approximately six miles. The speediest ships could be kept under constant fire for close to an hour; slower ones, even longer. In addition to those, the batteries at Aquia Creek still existed. At Boyd's Hole and above and below it and opposite Maryland Point and Sandy Point, the Confederates on occasion installed annoying field batteries which increased the danger of a Potomac River passage. The whole Confederate line was more solidly formed by the fall; Johnston had pulled

Use of a calcium light by a ship of the Potomac Flotilla to view the Evansport battery at night. *Leslie's Illustrated Weekly,* courtesy Roger Cohen, Jr.

back his outposts and established himself at Centreville in October. The Confederate Army was also reorganized in October with the creation of the Department of Northern Virginia under General Joseph Johnston. Three Districts were created: Potomac, Aquia, and Valley. The troops in Whiting's command belonged to the Potomac District while those at Aquia Creek, Evansport, Shipping Point and Brooke Station came under General Theophilus Holmes in the Aquia District.

Disgusted at the turn of events, even though they were anticipated for months, Commander Craven wrote Gideon Welles, "So long as the batteries stand at Shipping Point and Evansport the navigation of the Potomac will be effectually closed. To attempt to reduce them with the vessels under my command would be vanity. Had our army occupied the points opposite, as I have suggested in previous communications, this insult would not have been perpetrated." On the 17th of October from the *Harriet Lane,* the new flagship of the Flotilla, Craven recommended that no more government stores be sent to Washington via the Potomac until the batteries were removed or silenced. Captain Mitchell of the *Mount Vernon,* who had returned to Washington, reported that there were between thirty and forty ships with government stores such as hay, oats, potatoes, lumber and coal waiting to come up the Potomac, plus oyster boats lying off Smith's Point, Maryland. They were being detained by the Flotilla. On the orders of Commander Craven, all of the ships carrying supplies for the government were directed to leave the Potomac and go to Baltimore. Led by the *Thomas Swann* and *Virginia,* transports from New York, they proceeded to Locust Point to unload. Simultaneously, the Baltimore and Ohio Railroad was notified by the government to have all its available stock ready to transport the supplies to Washington. Mr. J.D. McKean, the B. and O. agent at the point, was ready with a large number of laborers to assist in transferring the stores from the ships to the railroad cars. William P. Smith, the B. and O.'s Master of Transportation, was there to supervise. On the 31st Craven wrote that it was his opinion that no vessel drawing more than eight feet of water could pass up or down the Potomac with the number of batteries in existence. Captains of light draft boats, carrying other than government orders, were allowed to run the batteries if they desired but only after a ship of the Flotilla warned them that they did so at their own risk. Merchants from southern Maryland petitioned the Navy Department for permission to allow ships to go up as far as Smith's Point to pick up produce for market. They complained that the blockade was causing them inconvenience and pecuniary embarrassment. The exception was made.

Commander Craven anticipated that the turn of events would hurt his career. Feeling that the public would accuse him of dereliction of duty, he requested that he "be detached from the command and appointed to some sea going vessel." He was officially detached on November 29, 1861, and assigned to the sloop of war, *Brooklyn*. Before leaving he made a last hope suggestion:

> In view of the utter uselessness of the Potomac Flotilla for the further protection of the river, I feel it my duty to respectfully suggest for consideration of the Department that the guns of all vessels be landed at Mattawoman Creek and mounted upon Stump Neck. . . . Then, with the aid of as many heavy siege mortars as are available, we might, by concentrating our fire upon one battery at a time, be enabled to drive the enemy from his position on the opposite bank of the river. . . . I am wholly ignorant of the proper management of such an operation, but if entrusted to a competent officer I should have no doubt that it would result to our advantage.

The suggestion was rejected. Craven was temporarily replaced by Lieutenant Commanding A. D. Harrell. When he received an assignment to command the gunboat, *Miami*, out of Philadelphia, Lieutenant Commanding R. H. Wyman replaced him as the permanent commander of the Potomac Flotilla. He assumed command on December 5th; the *Harriet Lane* continued to be the flagship. When the *Harriet Lane* was sent to the Gulf of Mexico in mid-February, 1862, the *Yankee* became the flagship again.

United States Steamer *Harriet Lane.* (O. R. Navies.)

CHAPTER VIII

THE EFFECT ON WASHINGTON

That such a serious danger to the Capital of the United States had been foreseen, yet allowed, struck everyone with amazement. People found it difficult to understand how Washington could become the only besieged Northern city when an army of two hundred thousand men, armed, equipped and in an apparent state of readiness were encamped in the city awaiting orders and a Flotilla of the U.S. Navy was on the Potomac River. General McClellan, with whom a major share of the responsibility rested, was not at all surprised. His engineers conditioned him to expect it. He denied, however, that he was at all to blame. He claimed responsibility rested with the Navy. He was certain that the batteries could have been prevented if a large enough naval force had been present on the Potomac from the beginning of the war.

Once the batteries were an accomplished fact, it was taken for granted that the War Department would do something, especially since their existence was so distressing to the President. In addition, it was feared that with the help of the *Page* and small boats and scows that had been accumulated on the Virginia side in August, the Confederates might attempt to land troops in Maryland and stir up an insurrection. More in response to the latter possibility than to the actual existence of the batteries, McClellan sent General Joseph Hooker's Division with eight thousand men and three field batteries of eighteen guns to southern Maryland. They left Bladensburg, Maryland, on October 24th. Some arrived at the Posey Plantation near Budd's Ferry at 8 p.m. Saturday the 26th; others, the following day. Ten camps, two to six miles apart, were established as far down

89

U.S. Government depot and boat landing at Rum Point on Mattawoman Creek, Maryland. *Official and Illustrated War Record,* courtesy Fort Ward Museum.

the Potomac as Port Tobacco. They were generally one half to a mile in from the shore and supplies reached them via the river to Rum Point on Mattowoman Creek. Pickets patrolled the areas between the camps and the river bank. On occasions, when the air was calm, pickets on both sides of the Potomac taunted each other with insults. An account of one of these conversations was sent to a Little Rock Arkansas newspaper by a member of the First Arkansas Regiment at Evansport.

> There are a good many Yankees opposite here. . . . Last week some of our men had a conversation with them across the river. They asked if we were not nearly starved. Our boy answered that we had enough to live on until we cleaned them out. He then dared the Yankees to meet his group in the middle of the river, although they were two to one. The Yankees said they were going into winter quarters at Richmond. Our boys asked what route they would take—through Manassas Junction, maybe? They did not answer and conversation ended.

Captain William P. Townsend, Company C, Fourth Texas Infantry stationed near the Potomac between Freestone Point and Cockpit Point wrote his wife on November 7, 1861: "There is a large body of the enemy on the other side of the river. We can see their camp fires at night and in fact the fighters frequently converse with each other. Shots are everyday passed across the river. So you see we have something to diversify the eternal monotony of camp life."

The pickets kept the camps in Hooker's Division in constant communications with one another; a telegraph line kept the Division in touch with Washington. One of the more popular camps, "Camp Hooker," in honor of the General, was located at Budd's Ferry. Budd's Ferry, used to be a flatboat or rowboat ferry from the Widow Budd's house to the mouth of Quantico Creek. Since the rebel guns pointed directly at it, Mrs. Budd left her house on the river bank. The officers and men of the artillery unit used it to warm themselves and their coffee. They also helped themselves to the clapboards and

Federal picket on the Potomac opposite the Confederate batteries. *Illustrated London News*, courtesy Hensley Gallery.

flooring to make their bunks. When the Division was withdrawn from southern Maryland, the remainder of the Budd house was burned.

The Union soldiers at first were shocked by the inordinate number of widows residing in southern Maryland. They were exceedingly sympathetic and solicitious to the women thinking that some dread disease had deprived them of husbands and fathers for their children. In quick time the soldiers realized that they were being duped. The majority of the ladies were not widows at all but wives of Confederate soldiers. By calling themselves widows they thought they could save their lands from being confiscated by the U.S. Government for their husbands' actions.

Hooker established his Division headquarters in a small grove near Chicamuxen Church and called it "Camp Baker." The Division was strengthened during the winter particularly by the arrival in December of the New Jersey regiments. By February Hooker's Division consisted of General Daniel Sickles' Brigade, First through Fifth Excelsiors (Seventieth, Seventy-first, Seventy-second, Seventy-third and Seventy-fourth New York Volunteers), Colonel Robert Cowdin's Brigade of the First and Eleventh Massachusetts, Twenty-sixth Pennsylvania, Second New Hampshire and Third Indiana Cavalry, and Colonel Samuel H. Starr's Fifth through Eighth New Jersey Volunteers.

Surveys were made along the Maryland shore by Captain Robert S. Williamson of the U. S. Topographical Engineers of sites for Union batteries. After his reconnaissance of the Potomac in September, General Barnard, the Army's Chief Engineer, recommended "if we cannot take the batteries, we can counter batter them—that is, we can on Stump Neck and Budd's Ferry establish superior batteries to his, and it is probable we can so molest him on all points where his batteries could be effectually treated as to cause him to abandon his efforts." The best location was found to be 1/3 of a mile below the house at Budd's Ferry. The point selected was twenty feet above the water and directly opposite the Confederate batteries

Camp of the 8th New Jersey Volunteers near Mattawoman Creek, Charles County, Maryland. Courtesy Library of Congress.

Guard house of the Second New Hampshire Regiment, Charles County, Maryland. *A History of the Second New Hampshire Volunteer Infantry.*

Quarters of the butcher, Second New Hampshire Regiment, Charles County, Maryland. *A History of the Second New Hampshire Volunteer Infantry.*

at Shipping Point and Evansport. Construction was begun on November 11, 1861. The battery contained two rifled Parrott guns. Its effectiveness was attested to by Brigadier General Samuel B. French who was ordered to Evansport on November 13th to replace General Trimble as commander of the batteries and defenses in the area. He complained to headquarters in Richmond that the open areas between the batteries at Evansport could be crossed only with difficulty under daily fire and that four men had been wounded, two severely. Private Samuel H. Williams, Company I, First Arkansas Regiment, complimented the Union gunners on their accuracy in an article submitted to the *Washington* (Arkansas) *Telegraph:*

> Not a day passes that does not witness an artillery duel between our gunners and the enemy. At times the cannonading becomes quite spirited, and the shells fall thick and fast on both sides. The Yankees, I must accord them the credit to say, shoot well. Their bombs often explode in and over our batteries. Notwithstanding this, they have thus far done us little damage. Out of the innumerable shots they have aimed at us, not a man on our side has been killed, and but three or four wounded.

Eugen O. Perry, Company E, of the First Texas Regiment, also attested to their accuracy in a letter to his brother, Will: "The enemy have excellend [*sic*] gunners at their batteries that is they shoot very well. . . . The enemy threw a bomb at some of our men on the beach. . . . It fell in the water very near them, but did not burst. One of the men has the bomb now in camp." Hooker's field artillery was used on the Maryland shore opposite the batteries and some earthworks were put up at Glymont in the vicinity of Indian Head to prevent the rebels from erecting a battery at High Point.

Neither the occupation of the Maryland shore by Hooker's Division nor the establishment of counter batteries alleviated the condition on the Potomac. Just as the Southern seaports were beginning to suffer under the Union blockade, Washington was feeling the effects of the Confederate strangulation of the Potomac. The newspapers could no longer boast of an unprecedented number of ships. Washington, which had been proud of its busy wharves and twenty new storehouses, saw its trade drop off to almost nothing. Prior to the outbreak of the war the population of the city never exceeded sixty thousand. By the time the blockade was established, this was augmented by an army of two hundred thousand soldiers and forty thousand horses. Like all armies of that size, it drew a variety of followers such as contractors, inventors, correspondents and artists. Con men, petty thieves, pickpockets and gamblers lived off the crowds. To entertain the soldiers there were dancers, singers, comedians, and vendors of anything that could be sold. Whores plied their trade on the unpaved streets followed by men like Drs. Schuman and LaBonta who offered permanent cures for diseases of a private nature. Even the embalmers set up shop. In December, Congress began a new session. Senators, Congressmen and all their assistants, secretaries, clerks, lobbyists, etc., whose presence they considered so absolutely essential to the smooth operation of the United States Government, took up residence in Washington. These thousands and thousands of people had to rely on imports for their essentials. When the Potomac was closed, most things Washington needed had to be brought in by rail from Baltimore. That put a tremendous strain on the Baltimore and Ohio Railroad, the details of which will be discussed below.

Every resident of the Capital immediately felt the effects of the blockade through a general increase in commodity prices and the lack of some less essential provisions. With winter setting in the principal necessities of life were coal, wood and food. Prior to the blockade, fuel dealers, both coal and wood, were apprehensive about their ability to meet the demand and raised their prices. After it, the prices became astronomical. One has to understand the peculiar situation that existed in Washington with regard to fuel, even before the Army arrived, to realize the seriousness of the situation. The Capital was a seasonal city, the season based not on the weather but on Congress. The length of the sessions was indefinite; clerks were

Pennsylvania Avenue. Courtesy Library of Congress.

poorly paid and their jobs insecure; and the appointment seekers were often unemployed. Consequently, men rarely brought their families with them and generally lived in single rooms. In winter the chief means of providing heat was wood and each room had its own individual fireplace or stove. In practically every other square there was a wood dealer serving the numerous boarding houses. The trains, after the Potomac was closed, could not meet the demand for fuel. The *Daily National Intelligencer* on December 3, 1861, expressed its hope that ships carrying fuel would try to run the blockade to increase the city's supply and thereby lower the price. George T. Stevens, a surgeon with the 6th New York Regiment, camped on Meridian Hill, told of the Army's problems. "The Government was paying enormous prices for fuel consumed by the army because the Potomac was closed and all wood had to be brought by rail from sparsely wooded districts in Maryland. Washington was in fact a beleaguered city." The Sixth, like many other regiments, was not camped in a public building. Wood was needed to build shelters for the winter and to make corrals for the horses. Since boards for construction were non-existent, the soldiers cut down the city's trees for building as well as firewood.

Forage for the Army horses and mules was also in short supply. The animals were on short allowances. The countryside for miles around was scoured. One of the reasons for the Union's expedition to Dranesville, Virginia, which resulted in a skirmish with Confederate forces, was to gather forage. Wagon loads were brought back to Washington. General James S. Wadsworth, a Brigade Commander in General McDowell's Division, testified about the shortage before a Congressional Committee. He said, "It all comes over the railroad from Baltimore, except for a little now and then by a vessel which may run the blockade. There is a little gathered up in the country here, but it is a very small percentage of the whole amount. The supply is very short. As many as ten days of the twenty we have had no hay," except what was gathered by the soldiers. It was highly questionable that a military expedition could have been undertaken with insufficient food for the horses.

Food for Washington's many people was a number one priority. The Baltimore and Ohio did an adequate job keeping the city's residents fed. Basic necessities like flour, meat and vegetables were available but at a higher price and at times in limited quantities. Those special little extras that made one's dinner or menu something to rave about were non-existent.

One item that the city's residents consumed in abundance was oysters. Peddlers sold them on street corners, the Willard Hotel included them on its breakfast menu, and Harvey's Oyster Saloon kept twenty men busy shucking and scalding them for its many customers. Oysters were one of the few items unaffected by the blockade. The oyster boats were light draft vessels with fearless captains. Harvey's Oyster Saloon even advertised that its boats ran the blockade daily. The *Daily National Intelligencer* reported that at least Washington would have an abundant supply of oysters for Thanksgiving!

The most serious effect of the blockade was not the personal problems people faced such as higher prices and inconvenience but rather humiliation, not only for Washington but for the entire nation. It was inconceivable that the great Capital of the United States was a beleagured city. The *New York Tribune* called the situation:

> ... one of the most humiliating of all the national disgraces to which we have been compelled to submit. It has been most damaging to us in the eyes of the world. ... And it has been their haughty boast that they had maintained steady and effectual sway over the great channel of commerce through which immense supplies of our grand army of the Potomac would naturally have passed. Our own government has been subjected to very great expense and great inconvenience, in consequence of this blockade. The inhabitants of Washington have at times suffered from scarcity of both food and fuel from the same cause. If occasionally some vessel has got past the enemy's guns, it has been under the cover of darkness,

or at considerable risk, in the same way that
our blockade of the Southern coast is often
run by the Confederates.

The only factor that prevented the blockade from being
catastrophic was the railroad, Washington's only other link with
the North. The importance of Maryland's remaining in the
Union was brought home when the Confederates blockaded the
Potomac River. Had Maryland seceded, a complete rather than
partial blockade would have befallen the Federal Capital.

Washington's sole connection with the rest of the Union
from October, 1861, until March of 1862 was provided by the
Baltimore and Ohio Railroad. To a point known as Relay House,
eight miles south of Baltimore, it was double-tracked. From
there the line's main branch turned west and a single-track
branch road continued south to Washington. After the Baltimore riots, the city, for a time, was avoided. Troops were sent
over the Annapolis and Elk Ridge Railroad which was occupied
by General Benjamin Butler. The B. and O., with which it connected at Annapolis Junction, was possessed by the War Department—the birth of the U.S. Military Railroad System. From
April, 1861, until early in October the operation of the Washington Branch was under the joint supervision of the Company
and the Federal Government. Secretary of War, Simon Cameron,
appointed Thomas A. Scott, Vice-President of the Pennsylvania
Railroad, to be in charge of the railroad and telegraph between Washington and Annapolis on April 17th. This was a
blow to John Garrett, President of the Baltimore and Ohio Railroad Company, because Scott was a railroad rival. But then
again, so was Cameron; his family had controlling interest in
the Northern Central, another B. and O. rival. With some justi-
fication Cameron has been accused of bias in his direction of the
railroads. Scott's chief assistant was the twenty-six year old future "steel king," Andrew Carnegie. Scott remained in this position until his appointment as Assistant Secretary of War with
supervision of all government railways and transportation.

The complete operation of the line was restored to the B.
and O. Company. The loyalty of Garrett, its President, was

questioned at the beginning of the war. He had been a supporter of the Crittendon Amendment to the Constitution. But his real loyalty was to his railroad and he would do whatever was necessary to protect and develop it. Since Maryland remained within the Union, Garrett was pro-North. The pro-Southern sympathizers within the state held him responsible for their inability to seize or at least isolate the city of Washington. He received threats against his life from Marylanders and letters of warning from citizens of Virginia.

The war period placed greater demands on the Washington Branch line than any other time in its history. Even before the blockade, preparations for Bull Run resulted in the doubling of its tonnage revenues. Equipment and men were taken from the Main Stem and additional track and sidings were added in the summer of 1861. The blockade, which placed unprecedented demands on the line, coincided with the B. and O.'s 36th fiscal year which ran from October, 1861, to September 30, 1862.

Prior to the war the freight brought to Washington by ship was supplemented by eight freight cars daily. The Depot and facilities were more than adequate for the disposition of goods. Even though the line was expanded during the summer of 1861, it was woefully inadequate to be Washington's only means of supply when the Potomac was closed. A correspondent for the *New York Post* described the conditions between Baltimore and Washington from his personal experience on October 23rd:

> The long railroad trains are inconveniently crowded, and it is impossible for the overburdened locomotives to run on time. . . . The Washington Branch railroad from Baltimore is entirely inadequate to the work crowded upon it. Another track is needed upon this road to complete the line of double track now extending as far south as Baltimore. . . . As it is now, nearly every turn out between here and Baltimore is covered with freight trains waiting an opportunity to pass, and it is impossible to form a calculation as to the time required

for the transportation of freight. The rolling
stock of the road has been largely increased by
borrowing from the Philadelphia, Wilmington,
and Baltimore Road, and it is all out of pro-
portion to its track accommodations.

To increase its capacity the Washington Branch line under-
went an enormous and unprecedented expansion, costing approximately one hundred thirty million dollars. A wye to turn engines and additional side tracks in the depot yard and streets
were laid in Washington. A new enginehouse and tonnage plat-
forms were built. New sidings were laid along the route to Baltimore and a direct line was constructed to Relay House connecting the Main Branch and the Washington Branch to facilitate
traffic. Equipment was borrowed from other lines. To ease the
fuel shortage special coal cars were acquired and cars were built
designed specifically for transporting large quantities of wood.
The number of cars delivered at Washington during the blockade
often exceeded four hundred daily with the greatest possible
variety of supplies.

The engine mileage for the 1862 fiscal year showed an increase of 293,834 miles. The Washington Branch road earned
$778,416, a gain of $340,277 over the previous year. The effect
of the blockade, which lasted from October, 1861, to March,
1862, can readily be seen in the breakdown of income compiled by W. P. Smith, Master of Transportation of the Baltimore and Ohio Railroad:

Month	Revenues From Tonnage	Revenues From Passengers	Total Business
April, 1861	$ 2,481.48	$ 8,003.67	$ 10,485.15
May	4,023.58	11,183.52	15,207.10
June	6,240.41	24,961.00	31,201.41
July	12,974.03	41,542.35	54,516.38
August	15,680.72	37,192.70	52,873.52
September	17,702.32	34,150.43	51,852.75
October	24,719.33	44,509.74	69,229.06
November	43,250.64	46,936.28	90,186.96
December	51,464.59	50,328.94	101,793.53

January, 1862	45,878.36	31,729.49	77,607.85
February	39,599.92	27,407.78	67,007.70
March	30,693.37	32,409.97	63,103.34
April	13,176.49	26,928.29	40,104.78
May	15,655.72	25,959.53	41,615.45

The experience of complete reliance upon the railroad led Secretary Cameron in his *Annual Report of the Secretary of War* to recommend that the railroad be double-tracked between Washington and Annapolis Junction in order to be assured of abundant supplies at all times. It was done but not completed until December, 1864.

In spite of the war free enterprise still existed and some of the local freight companies such as Messrs. Gibsons and Company, saw an opportunity to rival the railroad. They organized horse-drawn wagon trains over the turnpikes between Washington and Baltimore. On some days there were as many as one hundred wagons making the trip. The Government rejected the idea but gave consideration to taking possession of the turnpikes and putting the roads and bridges in proper condition for Federal wagon trains. Although the freight companies got off to a pretty good start, the poor condition of the roads made the journey difficult and slow. When the bridge at Beltsville collapsed, the death knell tolled for them. The cost of keeping the turnpikes in good condition was prohibitive.

If Maryland had seceded, Washington's rail connection would have been severed. Then, like the castles of old, the Capital of the United States would either have been forced into capitulation or the Army of the Potomac would have had to mount a large scale assault on the Confederates to preserve the freedom of Washington, D.C. The railroad, however, managed the supply of Washington satisfactorily. Although it caused inconvenience, the blockade did not result in any catastrophic suffering. It did cause mental anguish and can be regarded as an early example of psychological warfare.

CHAPTER IX

THE WINTER ON THE POTOMAC

Life on the Potomac was hectic for the officers and men of the ships; those below the batteries had to depend on Baltimore for their supplies. The dismembered Flotilla was ordered to engage the batteries only if it could be done without exposing ships or crews. Dahlgren suggested plating the *Anacostia* to lessen the risk of passage. The first serious disaster on the river involved the schooner *Fairfax* out of Georgetown. It was bound up the river with a cargo of hay and cement. Tugs of the Flotilla often towed ships past the batteries. On that occasion the towline broke and the Fairfax was captured by the rebels off Shipping Point.

Another incident which occurred off Cockpit Point was an example of heroism and drew cheering spectators to both shores of the Potomac. A schooner carrying wood was slowed off the point by lack of wind about 8 a.m. November 14, 1861. Rebel field artillery on Cockpit Point (Possum Nose) opened up on the schooner making three minor hits and frightening the crew so much they dropped anchor and swam for the Maryland shore. The Confederates launched a small boat with about twelve men from their side of the river. They boarded the abandoned schooner and set her on fire. Just as they began to row back to shore a detachment from the First Massachusetts Infantry approached the burning boat. Cheered on by their fellow soldiers crowding the Maryland shore, they boarded the schooner, threw off the load of wood, pulled open the hatches and doused the fire. In the meantime the Confederate gunners, with encouragement from their cohorts, were placing shot and shell all around the boat. A section of the Fifth U.S. Artillery arrived with two 10-pounder Parrotts and began shelling the Virginia shore as the Massachusetts detachment towed the unfortunate vessel to a safe anchorage in Mattawoman Creek. On the Union side the damage was slight, one pig killed and one mule wounded. On the Confederate side there was no report of physical injury but there were some close calls and much mental anguish. At the first sound of a gun members of the First and Fourth Texas Regiments rushed to Cockpit Point (Possum Nose) hoping that the cannon fire meant Union troops were attempting to land. The Texas boys were aching to teach the Yankees a lesson in the art of warfare. Much to their disappointment such was not the case. In addition, a gunboat arrived on the scene and shelled the Virginia shore forcing the Texans to retreat or be hit. Many of them spent a humiliating night in a hollow behind Cockpit Point without blankets or food.

Aside from the batteries, the biggest threat on the river to the Federal land and river forces was the steamer, *George Page*, which the Confederates captured early in the war and renamed, the *City of Richmond*. She was an ordinary riverboat employed carrying passengers on the Potomac before the war. The *Page* was 128 feet long and very fast with only a four-foot draft. The Confederates mounted four 32-pound cannons on her deck, forward and aft and one long pivot gun amidships. She had a complement of about 150 men. As long as the Flotilla was at full strength, a ship was permanently stationed off Aquia Creek to control the battery and prevent the *Page* from stealing out into the river.

Ward formulated a plan for cutting out the *Page* in late June but the plan was frustrated when the *Page* was moved farther up Aquia Creek. On July 9th the *Page* again was anchored in the creek near the railroad landing. Commander Benjamin Dove fired at her with the *Pocahontas'* 32-pounder and set her on fire. The flames were quickly brought under control and once again the *Page* was moved farther up the creek out of reach.

After the ships left for Port Royal, it was impossible to keep Aquia Creek blockaded. On October 23rd, the *Page*

The Confederate steamer *George Page* in Aquia Creek. Sketched by Lieutenant Osbon. *Harper's Weekly*, October 5, 1861.

ran out and anchored on the Potomac under the battery at Shipping Point. The next day she crossed the river and shelled part of General Sickles' Brigade, which had preceded Hooker to southern Maryland, forcing it back from the river. The appearance of the *George Page* kept up the apprehension of a Confederate landing in Maryland and increased the hazards of transit on the Potomac. Instead of returning to Aquia Creek, the *Page* was directed to a new anchorage in Quantico Creek. A Union field battery consisting of two Parrott guns was built seventy yards up the river from Budd's Ferry across from the *George Page* to prevent her from returning to the river again. At four o'clock, October 31st, General Hooker directed the battery to fire on the *Page*'s smokestack which was visible from the Maryland side of the Potomac. Whether or not the ship was hit could not be determined. If it were, the damage had to have been slight; the ship was moved one hundred yards farther up the creek beyond the range of the battery. The existence of the battery kept the *Page* up Quantico Creek during the day but she was often taken out into the river on dark nights reanchoring either back in Quantico Creek or in Chopawamsic Creek.

A request to capture the *Page* from Quantico Creek was made by Lieutenant Foxhall A. Parker's howitzer battery. Commander Wyman denied them permission. He regarded their plan as impractical with little chance of success. The Confederates had moved the *Page* down to Chopawamsic Creek. From a deserter it was learned that the rebels anticipated an attempt to capture the *Page* and had prepared for it. In addition to the battery at Chopawamsic Creek, the *Page*'s guns were manned, guarding the narrow mouth of the creek and a field battery was erected to protect her. A large body of men was also stationed nearby. The *Page* was neither captured nor destroyed by the Union forces on the Potomac. She was a serious threat but never did any damage.

For the most part, the same could be said of the Confederate batteries. With all the guns they possessed, one would think any ship within range would have been blown right out of the water. We should have a long list of ships sunk; we don't.

Union field battery consisting of two 10-pound Parrott guns at Budd's Ferry, Charles County, Maryland. *Illustrated London News*, courtesy Hensley Gallery.

Occasionally a ship was hit but rarely was the damage serious. The *Harriet Lane* was struck on the port wheelhouse but such incidents were rare when you consider that the ships of the Flotilla passed the batteries day and night. Light-draft vessels generally passed under fire but safely at night. Regulars on the Potomac were the oyster boats and only one is recorded as being hit but not sunk. General Hooker commented that from his observations, "they are as likely to be struck by lightning as by rebel shot."

The heaviest concentration of guns was at Shipping Point, Evansport and Cockpit Point. Some of those originally installed at Evansport were transferred to the latter. At first General Samuel French, who replaced General Trimble as commander of the batteries, wanted to transfer all of the Evansport guns to Cockpit Point. He and Holmes did not feel that the Evansport batteries could withstand a combined attack from guns of the Flotilla and from guns on the Maryland shore but the plan was never effected. Evansport was reduced but not abandoned. Shipping Point was strengthened by French. To the ten 9-inch Dahlgren's already there (many of which probably came from the Norfolk Navy Yard) he added five or six heavy guns. They were mounted in circular pits so far apart from each other that no concentrated fire could be made on all of them at the same time. On December 13th while firing at a ship, a large Dahlgren exploded "making the earth tremble like it was in the throes of an earthquake." Two of the ten men on the platform when it blew up were seriously wounded and one was killed. A 32-pounder rifled gun replaced it.

It is thought that there were thirty-seven heavy guns and an unknown number of lighter ones on the Virginia shore. Hooker had little respect for them. "They do fire wretchedly," he said. "Whether it is owing to the projectiles or the guns I am not informed. From what was witnessed today and on previous occasions, I am forced to the conclusion that the rebel batteries in this vicinity should not be a terror to anyone. With a light breeze or a favorable current, a seventy-four line of battleships could ascend or descend the river at night with impunity."

Confederate battery at Shipping Point. *Frank Leslie's Illustrated Newspaper.*

Schooners passing Confederate batteries. *Illustrated London News,* courtesy Hensley Gallery.

Over 5,000 shots were fired by the Confederate guns during the blockade and few found their mark. The contempt in which the rebel gunners were held was exemplified by the captain of the *Mystic*, a commercial steamer, which ran the batteries in mid-January. When the vessel was directly in front of Shipping Point, which had the heaviest concentration of guns, the engine was deliberately stopped and the gunners challenged to hit the boat. Altogether eighty-seven shots were fired at it and after each shot, all of which missed, the crew jeered and laughed at the inept artillerists.

General French offered an excuse for one of his guns. "Sometimes," he said, "the Armstrong gun, at the same elevation, would not throw a shell more than halfway across the river; then again far over the river." The inexperience on the part of the gunners might also account for their inaccuracy. The guns at Evansport and Shipping Point were commanded by Naval Officers but manned and guarded by troops of the Aquia and Potomac Districts. According to a member of the First Arkansas detailed to Evansport duty, "there was no lack of volunteers. What better sport than this for bored foot-soldiers—heavy gun practice on hostile ships!"

One might think, however, that they would learn from almost daily experience and become accurate. Such was not the case. It was a fact that ships choosing to run the batteries usually made it. Officially, however, the river was closed to larger ships and those carrying Government supplies by order of the U.S. Navy. Perhaps most of those would have made it to Washington too, if they had tried.

One ship that it was imperative to run safely past the batteries was the *Pensacola*. A fleet was being readied under Admiral David Farragut to capture New Orleans and open the Mississippi. The *Pensacola*, anchored off Alexandria, was ordered to join Farragut. It was one of the largest ships the Navy possessed, three thousand tons carrying three masts. It was also heavily armed—twenty 9-inch and one 11-inch Dahlgren smoothbores, two Parrott rifles and two 12-pound howitzers.

The one serious drawback to the ship was her deep draft of eighteen feet and seven inches with a full load. Navigating the Potomac required a skilled pilot under the best of circumstances. It took two pilots, the cooperation of almost every ship in the Flotilla and the inaccuracy of the rebel gunners to get her past the batteries. At 7:30 in the morning she left Alexandria escorted by the tug *Pusey*, for an anchorage just below White House Point. Fastened to the starboard side of the ship, to protect her machinery, was a canal boat loaded with hay. The topgallant masts were struck. It was sincerely hoped the *Pensacola* could avoid conflict, but preparations were made for battle if one was forced upon her. A shell and a stand of

The U.S.S. *Pensacola* running the Confederate batteries, January, 1862. *Harper's Weekly*, February 1, 1862.

grape were placed on the carriage of each gun and sponges, rammers and handspikes were provided. New sand was thrown on the deck so sailors wouldn't slip during the battle.

Shortly after 3 a.m. the *Pensacola* got underway with no lights and absolute silence on board. The crew of the *Yankee* was individually aroused by the officer of the deck and ordered to battle stations while the *Pensacola* attempted to run the batteries. Every effort was taken to avoid noises that might signal the ship's coming to the Virginians. Confederate spies had already informed them that the *Pensacola* was due that evening. Fortunately it was a dark night; heavy clouds obscured the moon. As the *Pensacola* approached the *Yankee*, a light was hung on the *Yankee*'s mast. The lantern fooled the Confederates who were watching for the *Pensacola.* They thought the *Yankee* was the expected vessel and signaled her approach to the batteries down the river. While the Cockpit Point gunners watched for the light to come within range, the darkened *Pensacola* slipped past. They fired three shots down the river after they realized their mistake but it was too late. The *Yankee*'s beam served as a guide to the pilots. Below the batteries the *Thomas Freeborn* waited with another beacon beckoning to the *Pensacola.*

Although the Cockpit Point gunners were fooled by the ruse, the men on Shipping Point were not. Seventeen shots were fired from Shipping Point and Evansport in the pre-dawn gloom. Some flew through the rigging; most passed right over the ship. Without firing a shot the *Pensacola* had safely run the gauntlet. She went on to fight for New Orleans in Farragut's armada where she suffered thirty-seven men killed or wounded.

One of the most courageous undertakings of the Potomac Flotilla during that depressing winter was an attack on Cockpit Point in January, 1862. After considerable observation and some shelling, Wyman decided that the Cockpit Point guns could fire down and across but not up the Potomac. Based on this decision, he ordered the *Anacostia,* under Lieutenant Commanding Oscar C. Badger, and the *Yankee,* commanded by Thomas H. Eastman, to stand inside Cockpit Point to the northward and

throw shells into the battery. The attack was partially successful; some of the Confederate guns were almost immediately
abandoned. Two, however, were brought to bear on the ships.
One, a rifled 12-pounder which came from the Tredegar Works
in Richmond had just been installed to respond to an attack
from the north. The other was a heavy 80-pounder rifle which
succeeded in hitting the *Yankee*. The shot passed through the
port bow and lodged in a berth on the starboard side in the
forecastle. It slightly wounded one seaman. Two shells, one
from each ship, exploded under the 80-pounder dismounting it
and forcing the abandonment of that gun. The engagement soon
ended. Had it not been for the 12-pounder the battery might
have been completely silenced. The Confederates remounted
their guns and corrected the weakness of the position; the Flotilla did not attack it again. There appeared to be four or five
guns on the point. Captain Williamson on his map indicated that
there were six. The Confederates have not left their version of
the exchange or a statement of the number of guns mounted in
the Cockpit (Possum Nose) fortifications.

Confederate accounts of their activity on the Potomac are
scattered and often vague or exaggerated. The troops in the
Dumphries area, within hearing range of the batteries, were
convinced that the guns were more than making their mark on
Union ships. In a letter to his father written on November 26,
1861, William E. Duncan of the 11th Mississippi (Lamar Rifles)
wrote, "Our batteries are still doing execution when the Yankees
give them a chance. They do not pretend to run the Potomac
now so the Potomac is completely blockaded." Colonel William
Dorsey Pender, Commander of the 6th North Carolina Regiment, told his wife, "Our batteries a few miles below us have
completely blockaded the Potomac." Captain Townsend of the
Fourth Texas Regiment wrote his wife on January 11, 1862:
"We are only a mile from the Potomac and we can hear every
gun fired by our batteries at the shipping that attempts to pass
them—though the attempt is now seldom made unless on a
dark night or a very foggy day." General French, in a report
of January 14th to General S. Cooper, Confederate Adjutant
and Inspector General, stated that the river was lifeless except

for the eight or ten steamers of the Flotilla. In spite of their overly optimistic views of the success of the blockade, a truer accounting of their activities on the Potomac must have reached General Johnston. From his headquarters in Centreville he communicated to Jefferson Davis on February 23rd: "I believe that the guns on the Potomac have very little effect. Vessels pass the batteries at night without much damage." His con-clusions were correct. It was not so much the effectiveness of the blockade that caused the river to be closed but rather the decision of the Navy not to allow most ships up the Potomac, a decision based on the potential damage that the batteries manned by competent gunners could do. Washington, D.C., in fact, submitted to a blockade of its chief avenue of supply.

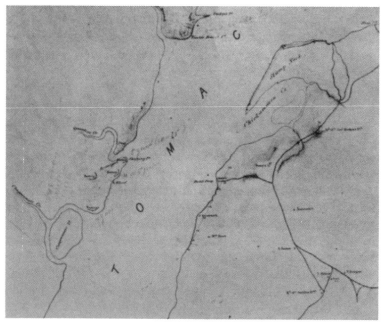

Surveys and reconnaissances in the vicinity of Budd's Ferry, Charles County, Maryland. By R. S. Williamson, Captain, Topographical Engineers. Courtesy Library of Congress.

CHAPTER X

LINCOLN ORDERS THE BATTERIES REDUCED

That the Confederate gunners were not deadeye dicks was no consolation to Government officials from the President on down. No one was in a mood to suffer the blockade any longer than was absolutely necessary. Responsibility for its removal belonged with the War Department and in particular, to General George B. McClellan who, in November replaced the aged General Scott as General-in-Chief of the Army. Simon Cameron, whose principal interests were military contracts and politics, let McClellan worry about the war. McClellan was an arrogant, vain man who liked subordinates and uncritical admirers. He was awed by his own personality and power and would gladly have replaced the "less competent" Lincoln as President.

McClellan had commanded the Army of the Potomac from July 27th and molded it into the greatest organization the nation had ever seen. The two hundred thousand plus men in the Washington area had great respect and confidence in their General. At his word they would have moved unquestioning into any battle. Knowing this was what irked so many people.

For all intents and purposes the Army was apparently ready. Perhaps it was not ready to engage a large group of well-trained European soldiers, but it was certainly prepared to meet another non-professional citizen army from the South. Reducing the batteries would have had an enormous effect. Besides ending the humiliation, it would have restored morale after the debacle at Manassas, appeased politicians, put off clamor for a general movement, brought a hero's acclamation upon McClellan and improved the diplomatic position of the U.S. as it sought to foil England's recognition of the Confederacy. But the General refused to give in to the many voices crying for a demonstration of Union strength. Later, in his book, *McClellan's Own Story*, he explained that "he did not regard the inconvenience resulting from the presence of the enemy's batteries on the Potomac as sufficiently great to justify the direct efforts to dislodge them." In his opinion a general movement, which was in the planning stage, would as a side effect, force the Confederates to abandon their line along the Potomac. He felt no need for conciliating politicians or citizens or for risking lives just to raise morale.

As the weeks passed, official Washington became more perturbed with McClellan's inaction. Applying the pressure to get McClellan either to reduce the batteries or undertake a general movement became a wintertime hobby. When Congress returned in December, McClellan's military supremacy was plainly threatened. A Joint Committee consisting of three members of the Senate and four members of the House of Representatives was appointed with instructions to inquire into the conduct of the war. The members of this Joint Committee on the Conduct of the War were Senators Benjamin F. Wade of Ohio, the Chairman, Zachariah Chandler of Michigan, Andrew Johnson of Tennessee; and Representatives D. Gooch of Massachusetts, John Covode of Pennsylvania, S. W. Julian of Indiana, and M. F. Odell of New York. They constituted a permanent court of inquiry with power to send for persons or papers.

One of the first persons the committee wanted to question was, of course, McClellan. On December 21st they sent him the following message: "Our Committee, at a meeting held this morning, unanimously expressed a desire, before proceeding in their official duties, to have an interview with you at our room at the Capitol." He agreed to meet with them on the 23rd. When the day arrived, however, he sent his regrets. He was too sick to leave his house with what was rumored to be typhoid fever.

With McClellan unavailable, they asked President Lincoln if he would meet with them to discuss the status of the War and allow the Committee to express its views to the President. General McClellan confided his plans to very few people. It was not even certain that he was planning a general movement never mind what the plan entailed. When the Committee met with Lincoln on January 6, 1862, its disillusionment with the General-in-Chief was unanimous. They recommended General McDowell replace him as Commander of the Army of the Potomac. At least, they thought, he would confer with the generals and communicate his plans of action. Mr. Chase, Secretary of the Treasury, came to McClellan's defense. The meeting adjourned with Lincoln agreeing to ascertain McClellan's views as soon as possible.

Lincoln, who was denied entrance to McClellan's sick room, was just as anxious for action as anyone else. He wanted a general movement of the Army but he wanted to be sure Washington would be secure in the face of the enemy's Virginia line. He also wanted the batteries reduced. Toward that end he decided to borrow the Army of the Potomac from General McClellan while he was sick. He took the unusual step of inviting some of the more prominent generals to the White House on January 10, 1862, for consultation particularly Generals William B. Franklin and Irvin McDowell. He told them that he was distressed over the condition of the country, a sort of general depression resulting from the Army's inaction. Secretary of State, William H. Seward, the Assistant Secretary of War, and Secretary of the Treasury, Chase, also attended. Discussion centered on the question of moving the Army at once and the route it should take to capture Richmond, directly via Manassas or indirectly by the lower Chesapeake.

Since no one was prepared to answer the questions involving transportation and supply, the meeting was adjourned until the following evening while McDowell and Franklin collected the necessary information. Postmaster-General, Montgomery Blair, was an addition to the next meeting at which the direct and indirect routes were debated. Again the meeting was adjourned so that more information on water transportation could be ascertained from Montgomery Meigs, the Quartermaster General, even though the majority of those present favored an immediate move on Manassas. This information, which was passed on to McClellan by Mr. Edwin Stanton, the newly appointed Secretary of War, who appears to have engaged in a little duplicity, hastened McClellan's recovery. Seward told the group on Sunday that he had seen McClellan. It was then decided the proper course would be to invite McClellan to attend the following day. The atmosphere at the conference was strained; McClellan was convinced that McDowell was intriguing for his position and had found support in the highest echelons of the Government. When asked if he had matured a plan for the Army, he replied in the affirmative. What the plan was he refused to say unless the President ordered him to do so. McClellan was in a morbidly distrustful frame of mind. Other plans he revealed to the Cabinet in the past had leaked out, he told Mr. Lincoln, and he did not want to jeopardize his newest plan. He was not ordered to do so. His attitude, however, worked against him. He was justified in being reticent but the image he conveyed was one of haughty silence.

McClellan was greatly disturbed by the way things had gone during his illness. He reflected later:

> The difficulties of my position in Washington commenced when I was first confined to my bed with typhoid fever . . . for some three weeks. . . . Up to that time there had been no serious difficulty; there were slight murmurs of impatience at the delay in moving, but all sensible and well-informed men saw the impossibility of entering upon a campaign at that season, and no party was as yet formed against me. Although I was in the habit of acting solely on my own judgement, and never told more of my intentions that was absolutely necessary, I always consulted freely with the chiefs of the staff departments.

He sincerely believed that a group of radicals led by General McDowell was trying to undermine his position with the President. While it is true that they opposed McClellan, there is no evidence of complicity in a plan to oust him. They just wanted him to do something. Revealing some of his thoughts to them might have been enough to reassure them but McClellan would not even do that. Despite what he said, he talked little.

Great pressure was applied to McClellan during the month of January. The Committee on the Conduct of the War grilled him on the 15th. The Secretary of War met with him. McClellan told Stanton that he was formulating a plan which would involve a campaign against Richmond via the lower Chesapeake. Stanton told him to develop it as soon as possible for the President. He also urged the General to take immediate steps to free the banks of the lower Potomac from the rebel batteries which were so annoying and embarrassing. McClellan naturally disregarded the latter. As long as the Capital could be supplied by rail, he did not regard the inconvenience sufficient enough to justify a direct effort to dislodge the Confederates when it was absolutely certain in his mind that they would evacuate the positions when he made his move on Richmond.

McClellan drew up his plan as he was instructed. Lincoln, who had thoughts of his own regarding a general campaign, rejected the General's. That Lincoln was ready to implement one became evident on January 27, 1862, when he issued his General War Order No. 1.

> Ordered, that the 22nd day of February, 1862, be the day for a general movement of the land and naval forces of the United States against the insurgent forces. That especially the Army of the Potomac, the Army of Western Virginia, the Army near Mumfordsville, Kentucky, the Army of the flotilla at Cairo, and a naval force in the Gulf of Mexico, be ready to move on that day.

> That the heads of the departments and especially the Secretaries of War and of the Navy, with all their subordinates and the general-in-chief, with all other commanders and subordinates and land and naval forces, will severally be held to their strict and full responsibility for prompt execution of this order.

He issued specific orders for the Army of the Potomac four days later:

Ordered, that all disposable force of the Army of the Potomac, after providing safely for the defense of Washington, be formed into an expedition for the immediate object of seizing and occupying a point upon the railroad southward of what is known as Manassas Junction, all details to be at the discretion of the Commander-in-Chief, and the expedition to move before or on the 22nd day of February next.

Lincoln preferred the direct route to Richmond for many reasons. Delays consequent upon the embarkation and debarkation of troops with all their equipment would be avoided; the Army in its movement immediately covered Washington rendering a large force in the Capital unnecessary; the batteries on the Potomac could be captured if they were not abandoned; and the Confederates would be cut off from the Shenandoah Valley, an important source of supply.

McClellan, whom Lincoln did not even bother to consult before issuing his war orders, stubbornly refused to give up his position. He asked the President whether the order for the Army of the Potomac was final. If not, he was ready to submit his objections and arguments for his plan of attack. Lincoln was willing to hear McClellan's views but demanded that he keep certain things in mind while expounding on his plan. These were contained in a letter written on February 3rd from the White House:

My Dear Sir: You and I have distinct and different plans for a movement of the Army of the Potomac—yours to be down the Chesapeake, up the Rappahannock to Urbana and across land to the terminus of the railroad on the York River; mine to move directly to a point on the railroad southwest of Manassas.

If you will give me satisfactory answers to the following questions I shall gladly yield my plan to yours:
1. Does your plan *involve* a greatly larger expenditure of *time* and *money* than mine?
2. Wherein is a victory *more certain* by your plan than mine?
3. Wherein is a victory more *valuable* by your plan than mine?
4. In fact, would it not be *less valuable* in this, that it would break no great line of the enemy's communications, while mine would?
5. In case of disaster, would not a retreat be more difficult by your plan than mine?

McClellan's position was contained in a letter sent to Secretary Stanton rather than Lincoln. He believed that the enemy expected a frontal attack and had prepared for it with concealed batteries and strategic concentrations of troops. The heavy rains that fell in January left the roads in poor condition. That made a commencement date uncertain and marching time impossible to calculate closely. If the attack on Manassas were successful and the enemy were defeated, certain objectives would be achieved. The Confederates would have to abandon the batteries along the lower Potomac and the line along the Upper Potomac would also be evacuated; the Union forces would occupy the field of battle; and a moral victory would be achieved. Richmond, however, would still be a long way off. If a sizable number of Confederates got between the Union forces and Richmond they could reassemble and fight again. If not strong enough to fight, they could still make the march to Richmond a tedious matter by destroying bridges and otherwise impeding the march over roads already in poor condition.

On the other hand, if the lower Chesapeake Bay were used as the base of operation; the condition of the roads would not be an important factor. The Army would be transported by boat and have only a short march to Richmond. The Union would have the element of surprise and all the secondary objectives would be achieved as the rebels concentrated to defend

Richmond, the capital of the Confederacy. To McClellan his plan possessed all that was favorable for a successful campaign; Lincoln's was weak in all aspects.

Although he was still not in agreement with McClellan, the letter had an effect on Lincoln's thinking. He directed McClellan to seek the advice of his generals. A Council of War was called of the twelve top general officers: Irvin McDowell, Edwin V. Sumner, Samuel P. Heintzelman, Erasmus D. Keyes, Fitz-John Porter, William B. Franklin, W. F. Smith, George A. McCall, Louis Blenker, Andrew Porter, John G. Barnard, and Henry M. Naglee of Hooker's Division. The generals were asked whether or not they would endorse McClellan's line of operation. By an eight to four vote they approved a movement by way of Annapolis, down Chesapeake Bay, up the Rappahannock to Urbana and across the country to Richmond. The question of re-opening the Potomac by driving the rebels from the batteries was discussed. It was decided to undertake the mission without disturbing them. The four dissenting votes were cast by Generals McDowell, Sumner, Heintzelman and Barnard. General Keyes voted for the general movement with the qualification that the Confederates be driven from the batteries on the Potomac first. General Barnard, the highly competent and very deaf engineer, had always opposed McClellan's plan. He thought that unless one hundred thousand men were left to guard Washington, the Confederates might try to take the Capital City while the Union forces were moving on Richmond.

It must be presumed, for lack of other evidence, that McClellan's letter to Stanton together with the results of the February Council of War, led President Lincoln to reconsider his Special War Order No. 1 of January 31st. While not formally revoking it, he never demanded its execution. Neither, however, did he endorse the other plan of action. He was not convinced that the movement of the Army to the lower Chesapeake would necessarily result in a retreat of the Confederate Army from Manassas and the evacuation of the batteries on the Potomac. He did see, as General Barnard had, a real danger that the Confederates would capture Washington once the Union troops left Annapolis. To approve McClellan's plan Lincoln needed assurances that the Potomac batteries would be destroyed either prior to or in conjunction with a general campaign and that Washington, D.C., would be secure. Lincoln's confidence in McClellan was deeply shaken but he kept him on even at a cost to his own personal prestige.

As is generally the case in times of war, the balance of power shifts to the executive branch of government. Congress has little power in the direction of a war. The Congress during the Civil War was almost impotent. It voted committees and asked questions without end. It achieved nothing of significance but it made its feelings known and they had to be respected if not heeded. The Joint Committee on the Conduct of the War kept the generals and cabinet officers busy fending questions on the general movement and particularly on the Potomac blockade which the Committee found most irritating. In mid-February Mr. Odell, one of the committee members, urged that the importance of breaking the blockade be stressed upon the proper authorities. In addition to the inconvenience and humiliation it caused, representations had been made to him by New York businessmen and United States citizens abroad of the disgrace they felt and the contempt in which the United States was held in foreign countries for allowing its Capital to be blockaded. A subcommittee was appointed to meet with Secretary Stanton to urge the immediate raising of the blockade. The subcommittee consisted of Senators Johnson and Wade. They communicated the Committee's thoughts on the Potomac blockade. Stanton confessed he went to bed each evening feeling shame and disgrace. General McClellan was in the building at the time and Stanton left to get him so that he, too, might hear the Committee's desire. Regarding the blockade, McClellan implied that some definite action would be undertaken in the next few days. The subcommittee reported back to the whole that the meeting was very satisfactory. The whole committee met again with Stanton at his home on February 20th and again urged an end to the siege of Washington. Stanton was very anxious that the blockade be ended.

After waiting for word from the Potomac for a week and hearing nothing, they again summoned McClellan. "Did you not," they asked, "consider it of very great importance to prevent or rid the river of the obstructions so that we might have the free navigation of the Potomac?" Again he told them he never considered it to be vitally important because Washington had an alternate means of supplying itself. Besides he added that the issue was "more a moral one than a physical one." In spite of what he said and against his better judgment, McClellan, in response to pressure was allowing General Hooker, during the month of February, to mature a plan

Reconnaissance by General Daniel Sickles in the Potomac River.
Illustrated London News, courtesy Hensley Gallery.

for capturing the Potomac batteries prior to a general movement of the Army of the Potomac.

From the time his Division was sent to southern Maryland, Hooker desired to cross the Potomac and capture the batteries. In February he came close to pulling it off. Preparations for an assault began soon after the camps were settled with apparent support from the Major General. In a letter to Adjutant General Williams on October 28th Hooker confessed he had no idea of the strength of the Confederate force opposite him and could not even find a deserter able to tell him. This declaration led General McClellan to engage the newly established aeronautic service on the lower Potomac. Balloon observations from Hooker's Division would supply information on the Confederate right flank that could not be ascertained otherwise, as well as more accurate information on the batteries.

Prior to his induction as director of the Balloon Corps, the twenty-nine year old Thaddeus S.C. Lowe had made numerous ascents from the Mall under the sponsorship of Professor Joseph Henry, director of the Smithsonian Institution. On November 10th he was ordered by McClellan to send a balloon to the lower Potomac. The balloon, *Constitution,* together with a generator and supply of gas materials, was placed on the balloon-boat, *G. W. Parke Custis,* and towed by the naval tug, *Coeur de Lion,* to Stump Neck. The *G. W. Parke Custis* was a steamer which used to ply the Potomac between Washington and Mount Vernon prior to the war. A broad deck had been erected on her hull to make her suitable for the balloon service. This trip was the first balloon expedition by water in history and it was a complete success.

Professor Lowe was accompanied by William Paulin, an assistant aeronaut, who had been selected to command the lower Potomac station. Hooker sent a detachment from the Seventy-second New York Infantry to help the aeronauts prepare for an ascension. The first people up on November 11th were Lowe, Paulin and General Daniel Sickles of Hooker's Excelsior Brigade. Their observations confirmed the information supplied

Balloon-boat *G. W. Parke Custis.* Courtesy Naval Historical Foundation.

A night observation of the Confederate batteries from the balloon, *Constitution*, using a calcium light. Courtesy Smithsonian Institution.

by the army and navy reconnaissance teams. Workers were seen on Freestone Point. Campfires were visible at Dumfries and Occoquan for about ten miles inland indicating that the rebels had a considerable force in the area. Anxious to obtain more detailed information of the works opposite his main command, Hooker ordered the balloon to Budd's Ferry, three miles down the river. It was moved overland to the area of Posey's house near Hooker's headquarters. The Posey Plantation, just under one thousand acres, was one of the largest farms in southern Maryland. "Big Dick's" house, which burned down in the late 1930's, had ten rooms, a big reception hall and a porch which extended along the length of the front facing away from the river. Posey's son reportedly joined the Confederate Army and Posey himself was arrested for communicating with the rebels in late October. He was subsequently released. A close watch was kept on him and his two daughters who were suspected of sending messages to the Virginia shore from their windows with mirrors and lanterns.

Lowe returned to Washington, to arrange for the disposition of his other balloons and to train assistants; Paulin took charge. Hooker needed the information that could be acquired from the observations in the formulation of his plans. Ascensions from the 12th to the 14th of November disclosed heavy batteries at Shipping Point and at intervals for four miles along the river. An accurate count of the number of guns was impossible; some of them were obviously masked. One gun was positively identified as the large Parrott rifled gun captured by the Confederates at Manassas. A continuous line of camps extended for miles parallel to the Potomac. These were the troops of General Holmes in the Aquia District and General W.H.C. Whiting's Brigade of the Potomac District near Dumphries. The most important ascent of the *Constitution* was made on December 8, 1861, a very clear day. Paulin took the balloon up to seven hundred feet. He was accompanied by a very able draftsman, Colonel William F. Small, 26th Pennsylvania Infantry who prepared a detailed map of the terrain opposite Hooker's camps from Chopawamsic Creek to Freestone Point, a distance of about seven miles. He showed the disposition of the Confed-

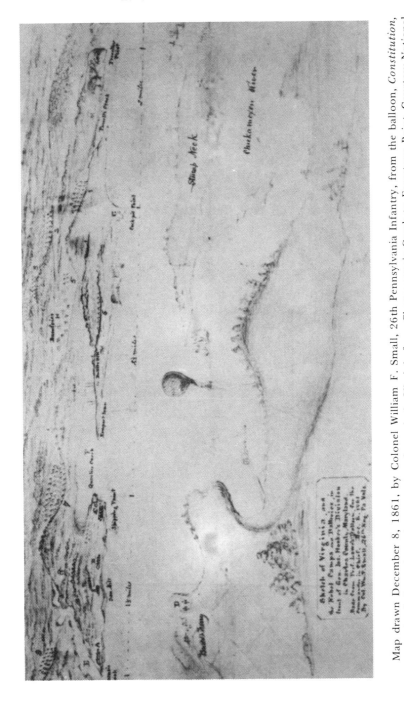

Map drawn December 8, 1861, by Colonel William F. Small, 26th Pennsylvania Infantry, from the balloon, *Constitution*, showing Confederate batteries, camps, and terrain in Virginia from Chopawamsic Creek to Freestone Point. Courtesy National Archives.

erate forces, batteries and topographical information. The camps were within supporting distances of each other and the batteries. By comparing tents and smoke of the Confederate camps with those of Hooker's, he estimated the number of rebel troops to be about 12,000, which was a pretty close guess. The accuracy of Small's map was affirmed by a Confederate deserter named Peterson, who was also a resident of the area surveyed. Whenever weather permitted observations were made. At the end of January, Ebenezer Seaver replaced Paulin, who was dismissed from the Balloon Corps by Lowe for engaging in a personal photographic business. The only significant change between then and February was an additional battery constructed about Christmastime on the outlet of Timber Branch to bear on Stump Neck.

One of the consequences of balloon observations was the enmity aroused by those being observed. The Confederates expressed their dislike by pot-shooting at the balloon with its large portrait of George Washington bulging on its side whenever it went up. The Budd's Ferry correspondent for the *New York Herald* reported an incident in which a soldier retrieved a 64-pound shell fired at the balloon that buried itself unexploded in the yard of the Posey house. He sold it to a civilian visitor from Boston who wanted it for an exhibit in the Massachusetts Capitol. Another one bounced off the Posey gate. Shells from the batteries often landed on the Maryland shore without exploding. The soldiers picked them up and sold them to souvenir hunters. At least one was reported to have brought as much as $20.

That the Confederates purposely fired at the balloon in hopes of bringing it down is also evident from their correspondence. From Camp Quantico E. O. Perry, First Texas Regiment, wrote on December 7, 1861: "The Yankees hoisted a balloon this evening just across the river. Our batteries commenced throwing bombs at it when quite a cannonading took place between our batteries and the Yankees batteries. What the result was I know not."

On October 30, 1861, Hooker suggested a plan of operation for the opening of the Potomac to Brigadier General S. Williams, Adjutant General of the Army of the Potomac. Without the specific information that the balloon would later give him, he was willing to cross the Potomac at night and occupy the high ground above Quantico Creek on the edge of the river. With field artillery of sufficient caliber, the Confederates would be forced to abandon their guns, the most effective on the river. The spot Hooker chose, he was convinced, could be defended against attack with the aid of the Flotilla. By shelling the rebels every time they tried to establish themselves, he felt the river could be kept open most of the time.

Through Williams, McClellan told Hooker he would give the plan serious consideration but more information was needed as to the ground, the approaches, and the character of Hooker's proposed landing. In one sense Hooker was discouraged; in another, he was encouraged because his proposal was not flatly rejected. With the information later obtained from balloon observations, Hooker was certain that the batteries could be stormed. Captain Henry Blake, one of Hooker's officers from the 11th Massachusetts, says Hooker was sure the high command would permit him to carry out an attack. The general submitted another plan of attack on January 27, 1862:

Colonel Charles Graham's 5th Excelsior, New York (74th N. Y. Regiment), being shelled by Confederate batteries while being reviewed by General Sickles. Courtesy Library of Congress.

I am of the opinion that the mode of attacking the rebels productive of the greatest results would be commence on the left of my line at Aquia Creek with one brigade, on the following morning to assault their batteries in front with two columns of a regiment each, the day following with as much of my division as I can cross, land at or near Powell or Neabsco Creek, advance on the Colchester Road, attack in the rear of the rebel batteries planted to dispute the passage of the Occoquan and open the doors for General Heintzelman to cross that river.

My reason for preferring to commence on the left are that at Liverpool Point I can embark the necessary force without exposing my object, can move to the point of landing without being observed, and can destroy their batteries and depot before it will be in their power to parry the blow, except with the force now in that vicinity. The effect of this on my command will be to inspire confidence. On the enemy, it will deprive a portion of them of their depot of supplies; with the balance it will threaten their communication with Richmond, and if it does not put some of them *en route,* and their roads resemble ours (very muddy), will compel their regiments to locate nearer their depots.

The primary objective in delivering an attack on my immediate front I consider should be to destroy the batteries in order to give us the free use of the river and not to give battle; for there are other fields equally accessible, affording greater advantages.

The Confederates expected Hooker to make a move against them. Jefferson Davis even proposed on one occasion that they attack Hooker before he had an opportunity to come at them. General Johnston dissuaded him, pointing out the impossibility of a retreat if they were defeated. That a Union

attack on the batteries could be repelled was considered doubt-
ful. General Richard S. Ewell of the Third Division of the Confederate Army regarded the position as weak; General Whiting,
who commanded the forces opposite Hooker's Division reported
"that the batteries could not be held against a formidable attack." If Hooker had been allowed to pursue his plan, the evidence suggests that the batteries would have been abandoned
even though the Confederates had a number of regiments in the
area to meet a Union attack on the Occoquan-Potomac line or a
concentrated attack on the batteries. In January 1862 these included:

Forces near Dumfries under the direct and indirect command of General Whiting in the Potomac District:

Fourth Alabama Infantry
Second Mississippi Infantry
Eleventh Mississippi Infantry
Sixth North Carolina Infantry
First Tennessee Infantry
Staunton Artillery (Virginia)

Colonel Hampton's Brigade:

Fourteenth Georgia Infantry
Nineteenth Georgia Infantry
Sixteenth North Carolina Infantry
Hampton's Legion (South Carolina)

Brigadier General Wigfall's Brigade:

Fifth Alabama Battalion Infantry
Eighteenth Georgia Infantry
First Texas Infantry
Fourth Texas Infantry
Fifth Texas Infantry

This is the only known photograph of the Texas Brigade in Northern Virginia. It was taken in a winter camp (probably that of the 1st Texas) near Dumphries in early 1862. *The Photographic History of the Civil War.*

Confederate cover addressed to: Colonel J. Johnston Pettigrew
at Evansport. Courtesy Brian Green.

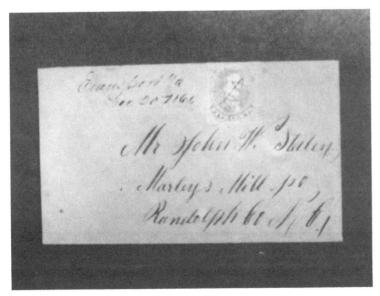

Confederate cover sent to Mr. John W. Staley from Evansport,
Va., Dec. 20, 1861. Courtesy Brian Green.

and a Detachment which included:

Reilly's Artillery (North Carolina)
Rives' Battery (South Carolina)
Shannon's Cavalry (South Carolina)
Thornton's Cavalry (Virginia)

In the Aquia District with Major General T.H. Holmes
commanding:
Brigadier General French's Brigade:

Second Arkansas Battalion Infantry
Thirty-fifth Georgia Infantry
Twenty-second North Carolina Infantry
Second Tennessee Infantry
Forty-seventh Virginia Infantry
Braxton's Artillery (Virginia)
Maryland Flying Artillery
Carolina Light Dragoons (Virginia)
Stafford Rangers, Cavalry (Virginia)

Brigadier General John G. Walker's Second Brigade:

First Arkansas Regiment
First Regiment North Carolina State Troops
Second Regiment North Carolina State Troops
Third Regiment North Carolina State Troops
Thirtieth Virginia Regiment
Cooke's Battery
Walker's Battery

With the pressure being put on McClellan in Washington, he
encouraged Hooker in the prospect that a directive to take the
batteries would be forthcoming, even though he personally opposed it. McClellan still hoped against hope that Lincoln would
change his mind and support his plan of campaign. He objected
to a limited attack by Hooker's Division and to President Lincoln's plan to take them as part of a general movement toward

A view of Budd's Ferry from the Potomac River. Prior to the Civil War it was a ferry landing. *Harper's Weekly*, November 23, 1861.

Manassas. Yet, he let Hooker and others believe an expedition across the Potomac was imminent. On February 17th barges for transporting troops were sent downriver. Thirty empty canal boats followed. Since it was impossible to cross battery horses, six naval boat howitzers with all the equipment for a landing party were brought to Budd's Ferry. They were to be crossed with the storming party. Men from the New Jersey Brigade, fifty to each gun, were detailed to learn how to operate them. Re-indoctrination was necessary because the operation of the boat howitzers was different from field artillery.

On February 23rd Colonel Charles Wainwright, Hooker's Chief of Artillery, received two Whitworth guns from Washington. They were rifled cannons with remarkable range, accuracy, and penetrating power. Solid shot was usually used in them instead of shell. Once in place, they were zeroed in on Shipping Point, and Cockpit Point. On February 26th Wainwright made three hits on the Shipping Point batteries. In addition to the new ordnance, a cavalry unit of the 3rd Pennsylvania Reserve was detailed to Hooker for the expected engagement.

Hooker again communicated with headquarters explaining that the balloon observations convinced him the batteries could be "stormed and carried." If the plan previously presented for doing so was not entirely satisfactory, he added, "I now have the means, with the aid of the Flotilla, of landing three brigades of my Division on the rebel shore and of demolishing the batteries" beginning with Cockpit Point and moving down river. "With six Dahlgren howitzers from high ground on the north side of the Quantico I can drive the rebels from the batteries at Shipping Point in two hours. The free navigation of the river will give us immense advantage over the rebels, particularly so long as the roads remain in their present condition, and the destruction of the batteries will in no way expose future intentions of the Major General in the conduct of the war."

Captain Wyman was in full accord and ready to participate in the assault. On February 27th Colonel Wainwright confided to his diary that "things begin to look decidedly like a move

the Ball enlarged!

Two of the Whitworth guns, which were presented to the U.S. Government by loyal Americans in England, were sent to southern Maryland for use against the Confederate batteries. They usually used solid shot and had remarkable range and accuracy. *Harper's Weekly*, June 15, 1861.

here. No orders yet, but undercurrents tend that way." That was to be the so-called war news that General McClellan had alluded to in his meetings with the sub-committee in Stanton's office.

The expedition, however, was cancelled. McClellan sent a telegram to his chief of staff which was forwarded to Hooker. "Revoke Hooker's authority in accordance with Barnard's opinion. Give Hooker orders not to move until further orders."

The excuse McClellan used for canceling the plans was an adverse reconnaissance report made by General Barnard. The consensus of opinion was that the plans would have been cancelled anyway and that Barnard's opinion was latched on to as the official excuse. The slaughter of Union troops attempting a landing at Ball's Bluff on the Upper Potomac near Leesburg, Virginia, had a sobering effect on some people including Barnard, who did not want a repetition on the lower Potomac. In his official report, vehemently denied by the Navy Department, McClellan contended that Hooker's plan would not have succeeded because the Navy could not give it adequate support. McClellan stated:

> The destruction of the batteries on the lower Potomac by crossing our troops opposite them was considered and preparations were even made for throwing Hooker's division across the river to carry them by assault. Finally, however, after an adverse report from Brigadier General J. G. Barnard, Chief Engineer, who made a reconnaissance of the positions; and in view of the fact it was still out of the power of the Navy Department to furnish suitable vessels to co-operate with land troops, this plan was abandoned as impracticable.

It was generally believed that Hooker's plan had been undermined even before Barnard expressed his opinion. To be successful the attack needed the element of surprise. That was not possible toward the end of February because news of Hooker's

impending assault had been leaked. Colonel Wainwright wrote
in his diary:

> Our expected move has all blown to the
> wind; it was to have been an actual move, a
> dash across the river to seize and destroy the
> batteries there and so raise the blockade.
> Sometime next week was the time the General
> intended trying it; but today all those who
> came down in the boat from Washington say
> it is talked of all over town, which of course
> renders a surprise impossible and quashes the
> whole thing. How it got out at Washington, I
> do not know, but should not be surprised if it
> was let out on purpose as a gentle way of let-
> ting the General down, his plans not being
> approved of.

Hooker was unable to hide his disappointment concerning
the turn of events when he wrote General Williams on the 28th:

> I received the instructions of the Major Gen-
> eral Commanding to suspend my movement
> across the river until further orders. Of course
> it is not for me to know or inquire for in-
> fluences at work about this suspension. I am
> permitted to state that almost every officer
> from Washington during the past week com-
> municated to me the fact that my command
> was to cross and attack the batteries and it
> was even announced in the *Baltimore Clipper.*
> For these reasons it ought no longer be con-
> sidered as an adventure of strictly a pri-
> vate character.

Lincoln, Stanton, Welles and the Committee on the Conduct of the War were furious, indignant and greatly disillusioned
with McClellan. People were openly wondering whether or not
he was capable of issuing orders. McClellan still hoped to win
support for his route to Richmond and schemed and stalled to
bide time toward that end. One major drawback to getting

Lincoln's approval was the continued existence of the batteries on the Potomac. Having cancelled Hooker's assault plans, he had to come up with another solution for destroying or controlling them. The author of the plan of action he accepted was General Barnard. The *Monitor,* the Union ironclad, being built at Brooklyn, New York, was nearing completion. Barnard suggested it could be used on the Potomac. With the assistance of a single gunboat it could keep alongside the batteries and control their fire so "as to keep the navigation sufficiently free as long as we require it." General Hooker, who had been informed of its possible use even before his plans were squelched, preferred an assault to destroy the batteries rather than just control them. In testimony before the Joint Committee on the Conduct of the War, McClellan claimed responsibility for the *Monitor* being completed ten days earlier than scheduled because he had requested it for use on the Potomac. Orders had been sent to Captain John Marston, Acting Commander-in-Chief of the North Atlantic Blockading Squadron, to send the *Monitor* directly to the Potomac River. Similar orders were sent to Captain John L. Worden of the *Monitor.* The latter's orders arrived two hours after the *Monitor* sailed from New York. With the situation as it was at Hampton Roads, Marston decided to ignore the orders. The *Monitor* went on to engage the Confederate ironclad *Virginia,* the ex-*Merrimac,* commanded by Commodore Franklin Buchanan, the former Commandant of the Washington Navy Yard, in history's first battle between ironclad ships.

Having run out of alternatives and fearing for his job, McClellan finally decided he could stall no longer. He wrote later in the year that he had undertaken:

> ... the preparations to carry out the wishes of
> the President, and Secretary of War in regard to
> destroying the batteries on the lower Potomac.
> Mature reflection convinced me that this op-
> eration would require the operation of the
> entire Army, for I felt sure the enemy would
> resist with his whole strength. I undertook it
> with great reluctance, both on account of the
> extremely unfavorable condition of the roads,

and my firm conviction that the proposed
movement to the lower Chesapeake would
necessarily, as it subsequently did, force the
enemy to abandon all his positions in front of
Washington. . . . The preparations for a movement toward the Occoquan, to carry the batteries, were, however, advanced as rapidly as
the season permitted, and I had invited the
commanders of divisions to meet at headquarters on the 8th of March to give instructions and ask advice.

That McClellan was making preparations was a deep dark
secret. He continued his habit of confiding in very few people.
He had begrudgingly won conditional approval for the expedition via Annapolis and transports were being gathered at
Annapolis to move the Army. There was general disapproval
of McClellan's plan and Lincoln, already distraught over the
death of his son, Willie, was almost overwhelmed by clamor for
his removal. Agitated by McClellan's attitude and barraged with
rumors concerning him, Lincoln sent for the General at 7:30
a.m., March 8, 1862. Lincoln told McClellan he wished to talk
to him about "a very ugly matter." It had been represented to
him that moving the Army of the Potomac out of Washington
was conceived with the traitorous intent of giving over Washington and the government to the enemy. Lincoln claimed the
idea was not his; he was just repeating what others had told
him. McClellan demanded an apology and a retraction. He
would permit no one, he said, "to couple the word treason
with my name." McClellan went on to tell Lincoln of the meeting of the Generals of the Divisions he had called for later in the
day to discuss a proposed attack on the Confederate batteries.

Distrust of the General had peaked. Lincoln apparently
was not completely reassured by the General during their discussion, for shortly after McClellan left the White House, Lincoln issued his General War Order No. 3.

Executive Mansion
Washington
March 8, 1862

President's General War Order No. 3

Ordered, That no change in the base of operations of the Army of the Potomac shall be made without having in and about Washington such a force as, in the opinion of the General-in-Chief and commanders of the army corps, shall leave said city entirely secure.

That no more than two army corps (about 50,000 troops) of said Army of the Potomac shall be moved *en route* for a new base of operations until the navigation of the Potomac from Washington to the Chesapeake Bay shall be freed from the enemy's batteries and other obstructions or until the President shall hereafter give express permission.

That any movement as aforesaid *en route* for a new base of operations, which may be ordered by the General-in-Chief, and which may be intended to move upon the Chesapeake Bay, shall begin to move upon the bay as early as the 18th of March instant.

Ordered, That the Army and the Navy cooperate in an immediate effort to capture the enemy's batteries upon the Potomac between Washington and the Chesapeake Bay.

Abraham Lincoln

When the generals met, they were under direct orders from the President of the United States to immediately reduce the batteries on the Potomac and to guarantee the safety of Washington, D.C., with a sufficient number of troops before the Army of the Potomac could be embarked for a battlefield in southern Virginia.

CHAPTER XI

THE CONFEDERATE RETREAT

Before the details could be worked out for breaking the blockade of the Potomac, word reached Washington that the Confederates had abandoned the batteries. On March 9, 1862, unusual fires were noticed on Cockpit Point and Shipping Point as the *Anacostia* and *Yankee* passed the batteries. Explosions were also heard. The ships began to shell the batteries; there was no answer. Wyman sent a telegram to the Secretary of the Navy expressing belief that the batteries were being abandoned. At 4 p.m. Wyman confirmed the evacuation:

> Cockpit and Shipping Point batteries have been abandoned; they have been shelled for an hour without reply. The enemy have set fire to everything at Shipping Point, and frequent explosions give evidence to the destruction of ammunition. . . . The *Page* I believe to have been set fire to and blown up.

Lieutenant Henslow, commanding a picket section at Budd's Ferry, noticed an unusual stir around the batteries earlier that day and was tempted to open fire on the large number of men who could be seen. Hooker had left standing orders not to, so he refrained. Later, heavy firing was heard from Cockpit Point. At first Henslow and his D Company thought it was the battery shooting at a passing steamer. Then the men began shouting and jumping as they realized it was the *Yankee* shelling the point and getting no answer. Company A of the First Massachusetts took a boat across the river to the Shipping Point batteries. Lieutenant Frank Carruth raised the

Camp Hooker on the lower Potomac, camp of the First Massachusetts Volunteers.
Drawn by William S. Henay, Co. D, 1862.

U.S. flag over the rebel cannons. The men returned to the Maryland side with a collection of souvenirs; shot, shells, bowie knives, battery apparatus, culinary implements and a Whitworth bolt Colonel Wainwright had fired at the battery a week before. Another Whitworth bolt was later found on a mantelpiece in a house one-half mile from Shipping Point. It was marked "Fired by the Yankees, February 27, 1862." Landing parties from the *Yankee* and *Anacostia* raised the U. S. flag over Cockpit Point.

General Hooker lost no time in getting out with the Flotilla to watch the shelling. McClellan's Chief of Staff, Brigadier General R. B. Marcy, ordered Hooker to cooperate with Captain Wyman in the destruction of the batteries if indeed they were abandoned or so feebly manned that no great risk would be incurred. Word of the evacuation took Washington by surprise. Lincoln and Secretary of War Stanton were elated; McClellan was still somewhat skeptical.

On the following day men from Hooker's Division including a New Jersey Regiment and some of the Massachusetts First were towed across the Potomac in a barge by one of the gunboats. Together with some officers and men of the Flotilla, they examined the fortified points and carried off the guns, ammunition and equipment left by the hastefully retreating Confederates.

On Shipping Point, which was the most heavily fortified, they found sixteen guns. Three of them, white oak Quakers (made of wood), were obviously designed to fool the balloon observers. Four other guns had burst during the winter. Care had been taken to destroy the remainder of the guns which had to be abandoned because of the wet conditions of the roads. They were loaded and shot wedged in them; lumber and logs were piled around and on top of the guns and set on fire. Two of the guns exploded but the others discharged normally because the shot was not wedged in tightly enough. The carriages were destroyed but the guns were saved for use by the U.S. Army and Navy. The English Blakely which was reported to have printed on it, "Blakely's Patent, Low Moor, 1861," was found loaded to

United States Steamer *Yankee*. Courtesy Library of Congress.

the muzzle with sand and a fire built beneath it. It was intended that the gun would discharge and destroy itself but the fire went out. The guns worth saving were tumbled over the banks to the beach where they were picked up by the Flotilla. Those too far inland to be brought to the river were disabled.

Colonel Wainwright was surprised to see how well the Shipping Point batteries were built. They were at least half sunk in the bank and from fifteen to fifty feet thick making it impossible for the gunboats to injure them. The magazines were cut into the solid bank. The gunners were screened by bomb-proofs, and their sleeping compartments sunk several feet in the ground. There was a good supply of cannonballs, cannister and grape-shot, and shells. Rifle pits and breastworks covered the areas adjacent to the batteries.

The Confederates had also tried to destroy everything at Evansport. Some of the guns were saved by the landing parties who removed the slow matches and trains of powder. They were recovered by the Flotilla. A few of the guns had obviously been disabled for some time. Many of the powder magazines there had been blown up.

Scouting parties were sent out to inspect all of the deserted Confederate camps. A large quantity of poorly kept regimental papers and private letters were found scattered about rebel quarters. They regarded these as indicative of a lack of discipline on the part of the Confederate troops and gross ignorance on the part of the officers. "Death to the Yankees" was the prevailing sentiment found in the private letters.

A description of the deserted camps visited by the contingents from the First Massachusetts can be found in the regimental history of the First Massachusetts. The author states:

> The deserted camps were found supplied
> with everything needful for winter-quarters.
> The houses were built of logs, with floors and
> roofs of board, some having glazed windows;

and one actually had green blinds. Their cooking arrangements were on the most liberal
scale; and the utensils good as to quality, and
plentiful in quantity; but houses, beds, and
everything else, in fact, were filthy to the last de-
gree. . . . If they had been kept neat or clean,
and laid out with proper regularity, they
would have been very creditable to their late
occupants; but they were filled with vile
odors. The houses were infested with vermin,
damp, and black with smoke, and most of
our men would sooner sleep on the ground
than in one of them.

   The rebels seemed to have lived upon the
fat of the land. Beef, pork, flour, bread,
salt, coffee, and c., were found among the
stores, not to mention whiskey, and a large
case of candy.

   In one instance, a table had just been set
for dinner, the meat was already cut, and the
cakes by the fire, showing, that from that
place the occupants were in too much of a
hurry to get away to stop for a lunch.

One of the interesting things found was a coffin warehouse
with twelve ready-made coffins and an order from one regiment
for twenty-four. Company rolls and morning reports found
among the rebel papers indicated a high mortality rate. From
one company thirty men out of seventy were reported to have
died. Some of the Confederate regiments were averaging one
death a day. Most of the Confederate regiments had a high percentage of men sick during the fall and winter. Dysentery,
pneumonia and measles were prevalent. One regiment, Colonel
Judge's Fourteenth Alabama which was assigned to General
French at Evansport from November until its withdrawal at the
end of 1861, was almost completely disabled by the measles.

   Some members of the First Massachusetts came upon fresh
graves which were well labeled with warnings against "disturbing the repose of the dead, and violating the sanctity of the
tomb." Ignoring the admonitions they began digging but in-

stead of bodies the gravediggers found new tents, clothing, well-equipped mess chests, and a variety of tools and other equipment.

Boats were brought over from the Maryland shore and loaded with loot of every conceivable variety from the batteries and camps. Among the things brought across the river were toothbrushes, buttons, Bibles, blankets, candy, tobacco, shovels and spades, wheelbarrows, chairs, campstools, powder and flasks, shot, gunsights, and cap boxes. When southern Maryland was abandoned for the Peninsula, Hooker's Division was directed to send its surplus goods to Washington for storage. Among the supplies sent in response to the directive were wagon loads of souvenirs.

In one sense Cockpit Point was an exception to Evansport and Shipping Points. Captain Frobel, who commanded the Fifth Alabama and a company of the First Tennessee at Cockpit Point, was determined that nothing should be abandoned that could be carried off. His personal possessions were loaded into a scow and sailed down to Chopawamsic Creek under the very noses of the Flotilla. The tents, baggage, cooking utensils, ammunition and battery equipment of the Fifth Alabama were removed. Powder was emptied from loaded shells and the shell and shot were buried. The guns were spiked but left mounted on their carriages. Two of the guns had burst in February; the others, which were in good condition, were thrown over the embankment and picked up by the Flotilla.

On the 14th of March General Hooker reported that "all batteries extending from Cockpit Point to Aquia Creek are utterly demolished." A rebel force had lingered at Aquia after the others retreated. Contingents from Hooker's Division continued to return to the batteries and abandoned camps until they left for the Peninsula on April 7th. They destroyed some of the battery sites at Evansport and Shipping Point and burned the rubbish. Landing parties from the Flotilla also checked out the batteries periodically. There is an account of two partially buried shells exploding on Cockpit Point during a reconnaissance by men from the *Freeborn* in October, 1862.

Third Regiment, Excelsior Brigade,

COL. NELSON TAYLOR, Commanding.

Camp Wool Apr 7, 1862

Dear Sister

I take my pen in hand to wright a few lines to you I receaved a letter from you March 27. Dated March 16 I was glad to hear from you in fact I do feel old since I have got to be Unkle there was one clause in your letter that I did not understand whenther you meant the name of the child or the parents of couzen annis we are still at our old

This letter was written by Lieutenant Hunt from Camp Wool, southern Maryland, on Third Regiment, Excelsior Brigade stationery. He tells of evacuation of Confederate batteries and complains that his regiment was not allowed to cross the river and visit the battery sites.

While the U. S. forces were engaged in the most serious tactical deliberations undertaken up to then to eliminate militarily the humiliating blockade of the Potomac River, the Confederates unexpectedly retreated. Their decision to retreat, which caught Washington by surprise, was made by General Joseph E. Johnston, Commander of the forces in Northern Virginia. Johnston was certain that McClellan would soon attack his forces on the first leg of a campaign to capture Richmond. His lines extended from Manassas with his right flank along the Occoquan and Potomac. He saw four possible routes the Federal Army could take. The first would be a repeat of that chosen in July when it suffered defeat at Manassas; the second would be down the Maryland side of the Potomac across to the mouth of Potomac Creek and on the Fredericksburg; the third and fourth were water routes, one to the lower Rappahannock, the other to Fort Monroe and then on to Richmond. As the Confederate troops were disposed, it seemed to General Johnston that the Union would select the route along the Potomac Creek and through Fredericksburg. That route Johnston considered the most difficult to defend against. The Union troops would be concealed on their march through Maryland until they began to cross the Potomac. If they got that far undetected, which was a possibility, the Union troops would be two days' march closer to Richmond than the Army of Northern Virginia on Bull Run. "I did not doubt therefore," said Johnston, "that this route would be taken by General McClellan." The location of General Hooker's Division on the Potomac reinforced his opinion.

Johnston had about forty thousand men in his command, much fewer than McClellan's two hundred ten thousand. He felt the number was insufficient if attacked and could see no possibility of receiving reinforcements. Realizing the Confederate vulnerability and expecting to be attacked any time after mid-February, he selected a new line of defense for the Army of Northern Virginia along the southern bank of the Rappahannock. From there the Federal Army could be met if it advanced from Manassas or through Fredericksburg. It would also be in a good position to join with other regiments in opposing the Union

Army if it attacked Richmond via the lower Potomac or Fort Monroe. A good defensive position was more valuable to Johnston than an indefensible one too far from Richmond.

President Jefferson Davis gave Johnston permission to begin moving to the Rappahannock in late February, 1862. He had hoped that the move could be made rapidly but heavy rains falling on roads already impassable in spots from a prior wet month caused numerous delays. Horse-drawn field artillery could not be taken over the roads; streams were so swollen they could not be crossed. That was the general condition of the land during most of the winter. The roads were so muddy and transportation so uncertain that General Whiting resorted to pack-mules and often to half rations. Drills and dress parades were often dispensed with. According to Nicholas A. Davis, Chaplain of the Fourth Texas Regiment, "the weather was so disagreeable . . . cooking, eating and sleeping constituted our chief employments." The Richmond, Fredericksburg and Potomac Railroad was overloaded carrying things that ordinarily would be moved by wagons or carried by soldiers. It was hoped that the roads would delay a Union attack long enough so that the mass of Confederate supplies, guns, ammunition and so forth collected in the Manassas and Dumphries areas could be gotten out.

On March 5th, however, Brigadier General W.H.C. Whiting reported he had been observing unusual activity in Hooker's Division on the opposite side of the Potomac. He was probably referring to the barges, canal boats and new guns that were accumulated for the proposed assault on the batteries. To General Johnston this "suggested that the Federal Army was about to take the field; so I determined to move to the positions already prepared for such an emergency, the south bank of the Rappahannock."

General Whiting received orders at noon March 7th to withdraw his command from Dumphries at daylight March 8th. The wagon trains and the sick were launched in the sea of mud as directed but most of the regiments maintained their positions until

A team is stuck in the mud on the road from Aquia Creek to Fredericksburg. *Official and Illustrated War Record*, courtesy Fort Ward Museum.

General French and his troops were at least two hours' march away from the Evansport and Shipping Point batteries. The North Carolina Sixth bade farewell to its winter camp by setting fire to its huts. The Fourth Texas, which left in the afternoon, was more conscious of its directive to retreat without letting Hooker's Division realize they were leaving. Since its camp could be seen from the Maryland side, particularly from the balloon which often went up, the cabins and tents were left standing.

For want of transportation and impassable roads a large amount of the personal baggage belonging to the various regiments was abandoned or discarded including hundreds of tents. It was easy for those sitting behind desks in Richmond to criticize Whiting for having abandoned so much. Under the circumstances it was commendable anything was gotten out. Whiting chafed under the criticism and wrote a letter defending himself and his men. He went overboard trying to show that the criticism was unjust, that not much, at least not much C. S. Government owned property, was left. Perhaps he was ignorant of the vast amount left in the Dumphries area and along the roads. He was aware that some private property was left. In his letter which was directed to the War Department but sent to General Holmes he said, "Most of the regiments also succeeded in getting off a large amount of private baggage. A portion of it was concealed with a view to recovery, at farms in the rear, and a portion given to poor and loyal people in the vicinity." Small contingents were sent back to reconnoiter the Potomac and Dumphries areas after the retreat. They often returned to their old camps to gather up as much as they could carry before returning to their lines. On some of these expeditions they were intercepted by contingents from Hooker's Division. In one such incident on April 2nd Luther Fassett of the Second New Hampshire regiment was killed at Evansport.

A large quantity of provisions, clothing, ammunition and guns was also abandoned at Manassas. Most of the Confederate positions in Northern Virginia were abandoned by March 9, 1862. An exception was Aquia Creek. While the rest of Johnston's army was moving to the Rappahannock, Holmes stayed on at Aquia destroying the railroad and facilities so the Union forces could not use them. All of the buildings were burned, track and ties for the first three miles were removed and the bridges over Accokeek and Potomac Creek were destroyed.

After Holmes left Aquia, Union forces occupied it with the objective of restoring the railroad to Fredericksburg in order to supply Union troops in Virginia, particularly those of General McDowell. The restoration was given to Herman Haupt, a railroad construction engineering genius. In less than three weeks, with few tools and unskilled workers, he laid the tracks and rebuilt the destroyed bridges. On May 23rd President Lincoln and some of his Cabinet members arrived at Aquia Creek by steamer. From there they went to visit General McDowell at his Fredericksburg headquarters via the reconstructed railroad. Lincoln is said to have remarked: "I have seen the most remarkable structure human eyes ever rested upon. That man Haupt has built a bridge across Potomac Creek 400 feet long and nearly 100 feet high, over which loaded trains are running every hour and, upon my word, there is nothing in it but bean poles and cornstalks."

At the Aquia depot site the wharves were restored and new buildings constructed. The railroad and facilities were used by the Union to supply its forces in Virginia at various times during the remainder of the war. General Ambrose Burnside, for example, used it in 1862 and General Hooker in 1863.

In March, 1862, General Johnston was complimented on a skillful movement in the face of the enemy. The applause, however, soon turned to criticism. The large amount of supplies destroyed in the retreat provoked everyone including Jeff Davis. No invasion of the South was launched from the Maryland shore; Hooker's Division destroyed or seized the abandoned Confederate ordnance; and the Federal Army occupied Northern Virginia but only after the Confederates had withdrawn. The *Richmond Examiner* accused General Johnston of retreating with no pursuer.

Herman Haupt's bridge across Potomac Creek which President Lincoln called a "beanpole and cornstalk" structure. *The Photographic History of the Civil War.*

Aquia Creek Landing as a Union supply base.
Courtesy Virginia State Library.

Information acquired by both General McClellan, U.S.A., and General Johnston, C.S.A., regarding the strength and intentions of the opposition was erroneous. General Johnston credited General McClellan with more initiative than was deserving and misinterpreted the Union activity along the Maryland shore as a certain sign that he would be attacked within days. On the other hand, General McClellan's estimate of the Confederate strength, based on his secret service bureau reports under Allan Pinkerton, was overestimated.

McClellan, who had strategic position, troop strength and logistics to break the blockade, must bear a major share of responsibility for the Union's acquiescence in it. He refused to either initiate or cooperate with the Navy in any action to open the Potomac River to Union shipping. Despite the fact that the blockade was a humiliating disgrace to the Federal government, a diplomatic embarrassment, and caused both the population of Washington and the Army of the Potomac great inconvenience, he regarded it as unimportant as long as railroad transportation to the city existed. His conviction that the batteries would be demolished as part of a general campaign was, perhaps, militarily correct, but after suffering a major defeat at Bull Run, the Union could have used a victory. With the resources at his command, and with the cooperation of the Navy, troops could have landed and held strategic points along the Potomac River. McClellan's failure to act shook Washington's confidence in his ability as a military leader.

The Confederate generals indicated that the batteries could not have been held against a combined U. S. Army-Navy attempt to take them. A general engagement would not have resulted. The Confederates' primary purpose at that time was to prevent a Union attack upon Richmond. Their strength was not great enough to concentrate their force along the Potomac River. It would have overextended their lines, leaving Richmond vulnerable. If a campaign against them had been launched, the Confederates would have abandoned the batteries.

Opening the Potomac River during the winter of 1861-1862 would have provided the Union with a great moral boost. It would have had a beneficial effect on the morale of the troops, and the spirit of the country, as well as bolstering the position of U. S. diplomats abroad in winning support for the Union's cause. In March, 1862, the mere threat of attack led the Confederate forces to withdraw from the banks of the Potomac. The river again teemed with commercial and military shipping and remained Washington's principal avenue of supply for the duration of the war.

APPENDIX

Although much evidence of the blockade of the Potomac River has been erased by time, some still exists. On the Maryland side of the river some of the camp sites used by General Hooker's Division and the earthworks for the Union batteries can be located in Charles County. The church at Chicamuxen is not the one that stood during the Civil War but its location is close to that of the old one. The old road, which once passed in front of the church, can easily be seen behind the present church. The Charles County Civil War Centennial Commission has placed a historical marker there commemorating the use of Chicamuxen Church by General Joseph Hooker during the winter of 1861-1862. Another historical marker is located near Budd's Ferry. The well and foundation of the Budd House, which was burned in 1862, have also been found.

The most well-preserved site associated with the blockade is Possum Nose in Prince William County, Virginia. At the time of the blockade it was considered part of Cockpit Point. The earthworks for the Confederate ordnance and powder magazine remain there today in excellent condition. The largest of these, fronting on the Potomac at the tip of the Nose, probably held three guns including the 80-pounder mentioned in the January engagement between the batteries on Possum Nose (Cockpit Point) and ships of the Potomac Flotilla. On either side of this large earthwork are two smaller ones. One of them must have held a single gun; the other, a little larger, possibly two. Behind these, running almost the entire width of Possum Nose, are winding rifle pits. If the batteries were attacked by a Federal landing party, the assault would had to have come from the rear. Possum Nose is a seventy-five foot hill with a cliff-like bank overlooking the Potomac.

Toward the rear of Possum Nose near the railroad tracks are the remains of the powder magazine. Many of the men stationed at the Possum Nose batteries also lived there in tents and log cabins. Hut sites, some with fireplaces, can be found in a few locations. Below Possum Nose on Cockpit Point, as the land begins to rise out of the marsh, were the remains of another battery, probably a field battery. They were destroyed during the writing of this book by the District of Columbia Government sanitary landfill project. An asphalt plant behind Possum Nose was constructed on the site of a camp.

No Confederate description of the fortifications on Possum Nose has been found but unlike other areas of Civil War significance enough has survived to give us a reasonably good picture of the point as it existed during the blockade of the Potomac River.

The most heavily fortified sector of the river was between Quantico Creek and Chopawamsic Creek in Prince William County. The area is currently within the boundaries of the Quantico Marine Base. The earthworks for the Shipping Point, Evansport and Chopawamsic batteries have all been destroyed. Shipping Point, for example, is now the site of a United States Naval Hospital.

Upriver on Freestone Point, also in Prince William County, the earthworks which were abandoned when Shipping Point, Evansport and Cockpit Point were fortified, can still be seen. They could become accessible to the public if the proposed County park on Freestone Point is approved.

Downriver in Stafford County are the remains of the once busy gateway to the South. Soon after the termination of the war a direct rail route was established between Richmond and Alexandria and the Richmond, Fredericksburg and Potomac Railroad terminal at Aquia Creek Landing was abandoned. A beach and picnic grounds now replace the warehouses, batteries, tracks and depot. Virginia Route No. 608, which leads to the site from Brooke Station, is built upon the old railroad bed. The road is so bumpy in places that the ties beneath the surface are in evidence today.

As obvious as the railroad bed are the remains of the old wharves where steamers and schooners used to dock. When the tide is out, the tops of the old pilings can be seen protruding from the water. If sufficient money had been appropriated to the Army Corps of Engineers, they would have removed these as they pose a threat to navigation.

Matthew Brady, the famed Civil War photographer, has left us pictures of what Aquia Creek Landing looked like when the Union forces occupied it. With these in view, it is easy to picture what a busy place Aquia Creek was as the gateway to the South in the pre-Civil War days, as the scene of battle in the first year of the war and as a Union supply depot in the later war years.

Not far from Aquia Creek Landing, at the end of Virginia Route No. 625, are the remains of the old railroad bridge across Potomac Creek. The stone supports, which can be seen on both sides of the creek, were used by Herman Haupt when he rebuilt the bridge the Confederates destroyed in their retreat of March, 1862. President Lincoln called it a "beanpole and cornstalk" bridge when he traveled across it because it was built from trees nearby without proper tools or manpower in an extremely short time.

The family estate of Dr. Abram Hooe was located on Mathias Point in King George County. During the blockade his home was burned by a contingent of the U. S. Navy in retaliation for his participation in Confederate activity and providing room and board for Confederate soldiers. The home was rebuilt and Dr. Hooe and his wife were buried on the property. In 1940, when the U. S. Government acquired the property, the remains of Dr. Hooe and his wife, together with the tombstones were removed to St. Paul's Churchyard located at the junction of Virginia routes No. 206 and 218. St. Paul's dates back to colonial times. The present structure pre-dates the Civil War.

Also located on Mathias Point was the Grymes home which was burned by Colonel Charles K. Graham's 74th New York Regiment and a party from the Navy's Potomac Flotilla when they landed on Mathias Point in November 1861. Until very recently the smokehouse, which escaped the torch, stood as a reminder of Civil War days.

Thousands of Confederate soldiers along with naval personnel participated in the building and operation of the Potomac River batteries. Many others were in close proximity ready to support them if it were necessary. Some of these troops camped at Aquia Creek Landing and at the batteries on Shipping Point, Evansport and Cockpit Point. Others camped at various places along the river. Despite the growth of Northern Virginia in the last one hundred plus years, some of the sites used as winter camps by these Confederate regiments in 1861 and 1862 can still be found—the legacy of an unfortunate war.

Chicamuxen Church, Charles County, Maryland.

Charles County Civil War Centennial Commission
marker for Budd's Ferry.

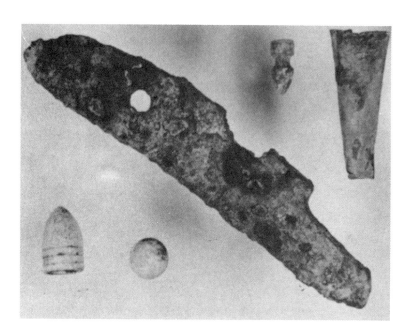

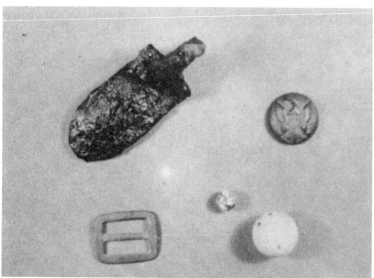

Courtesy Preston Law.

Possum Nose earthwork, Whitworth bolt and lantern stamped
BNY (Boston Navy Yard). Courtesy Sidney Kerksis.

Aquia Church.

Two carved cornerstones.

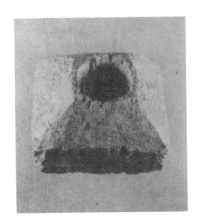

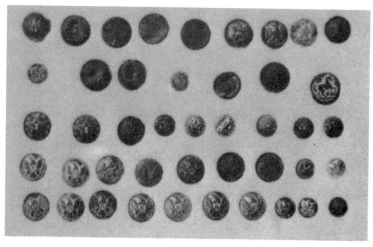

Courtesy Clifton English.

Courtesy Joseph Canole, Jr.

Courtesy James Durst.

Courtesy Clifton English.

Shell from the Potomac River. Courtesy John Ashton.

This gun was used in one of the Confederate batteries. After the Confederate withdrawal Union army and navy forces destroyed some of the abandoned guns by breaking the trunnions. Courtesy Quantico Marine Base.

Aquia Creek Landing today. Note pilings protruding from water.

Road to Aquia Creek Landing is built on old railroad bed.

The fifth largest of the named forts and batteries built for the defense of Washington was named Fort Ward in honor of Cdr. James H. Ward, the first U.S. Naval Officer of the Civil War to die in action. The fort has been restored by the city of Alexandria and functions today as a park and Civil War Museum.

BIBLIOGRAPHY

Unpublished Material

Camp Newspaper of the Eighteenth Georgia Infantry Regiment. The Robert W. Woodruff Library for Advanced Studies. Emory University. Atlanta, Georgia.

Civil War Letters of Fleet W. Cox. Company Commander, Fortieth Virginia Regiment. University of Virginia Library, Collection No. 4380. University of Virginia. Charlottesville, Virginia.

Diary of Colonel Charles S. Wainwright, 1861-1865. The Huntington Library. San Marino, California.

Diary of Oscar J. Downs. Confederate Research Center. Hill Junior College. Hillsboro, Texas.

Diary of Joseph B. Polley. Confederate Research Center. Hill Junior College. Hillsboro, Texas.

General and Special Orders of General W. H. C. Whiting's Command, September 1861-February 1862. Record Group 109. Washington: The National Archives.

General Orders and Circulars. General W. H. C. Whiting's Command, February-July, 1862. Record Group 109. Washington: The National Archives.

Guinn, R.A. "History of Important Movements and Incidents of the Newton Rifles." Manuscript. (No date.) Confederate Research Center. Hill Junior College. Hillsboro, Texas.

Hanks, O. T. "History of Captain B. F. Benton's Company, 1861-1865." Manuscript, 1921. Confederate Research Center. Hill Junior College. Hillsboro, Texas.

Headquarters, Virginia Forces, Letters Sent, April-November, 1861. Record Group 109. Washington: The National Archives.

John Adolphus Dahlgren Papers. Manuscript Division. Washington: The Library of Congress.

Journal of Stephen C. Rowan, 1845-1869. Manuscript Division. Washington: The Library of Congress.

Letters of Tacitus T. Clay. Confederate Research Center. Hill Junior College. Hillsboro, Texas.

Letters of Samuel Tine Owen. Confederate Research Center. Hill Junior College. Hillsboro, Texas.

Letters of William P. Townsend. Confederate Research Center. Hill Junior College. Hillsboro, Texas.

Letters of Dugat Williams. Confederate Research Center. Hill Junior College. Hillsboro, Texas.

Memoirs of Thaddeus S. C. Lowe. Washington: The Smithsonian Institution.

N. H. R. Dawson Papers. Southern Historical Collection. University of North Carolina Library. Chapel Hill, North Carolina.

Naval Records Collection of the Office of Naval Records and Library. Record Group 45. File for Area 7 (M623, Roll 412). Washington: The National Archives.

Naval Records Collection of the Office of Naval Records and Library. Record Group 45. Subject File 1861-1865. Washington: The National Archives.

Papers of Gideon Welles. Manuscript Division. Washington: The Library of Congress.

Records of the Confederate States of America. Records of the Navy Department. Manuscript Division. Washington: The Library of Congress.

Register, Letters Received, Virginia Forces, July-November, 1861. Record Group 109. Washington: The National Archives.

Robert Garrett Family Papers. Manuscript Division. Washington: The Library of Congress.

Special War Orders of General W. H. C. Whiting's Command, February-July, 1862. Record Group 109. Washington: The National Archives.

Telegram Accounts. Record Group 109. Washington: The National Archives.

Official Records and Reports

A Compilation of the Messages and Papers of the Confederacy. Nashville: United States Publishing Co., 1902.

A Compilation of the Messages and Papers of the Presidents, 1789-1897. Washington: U. S. Government Printing Office, 1897.

Confederate States Navy Register for 1862. Richmond: Enquirer Book and Job Press, 1862.

Cowles, Dalvin D. (compiled by). *Atlas to Accompany the Official Records of the Union and Confederate Armies.* Washington: U. S. Government Printing Office, 1891-1895.

Historical Statistics of the United States, Colonial Times to 1957. Washington: U. S. Department of Commerce, 1960.

Journal of the Congress of the Confederate States of America, 1861-1865. Washington: U. S. Government Printing Office, 1904.

Letter of the Secretary of War Transmitting Report on the Organization of the Army of the Potomac, and of its Campaigns in Virginia and Maryland, Under the Command of General George B. McClellan from July 26, 1861 to November 7, 1862. Washington: U. S. Government Printing Office, 1864.

McClellan, George B. *Report on the Organization and Campaigns of the Army of the Potomac: To Which is Added an Account of the Campaigns in Western Virginia.* New York: Sheldon and Co., 1864.

Official Records of the Union and Confederate Navies in the War of the Rebellion. Washington: U. S. Government Printing Office, 1897.

Papers Relating to Foreign Affairs, Foreign Relations of the U.S., 1861-1862. Washington: U. S. Government Printing Office, 1862.

Prince William County Land Records. Prince William County Court House. Manassas, Virginia.

Report of the Congressional Committee on the Operations of the Army of the Potomac. Tribune War Tract # 1. New York: Tribune Association, 1863.

Report of the Joint Committee on the Conduct of the War. Washington: U. S. Government Printing Office, 1863.

Stanton, Edwin M. *Report of the Secretary of War.* Washington: U. S. Government Printing Office, 1862.

Thirtieth Annual Report of the Richmond, Fredericksburg and Potomac Railroad Co., May 27, 1863. Richmond: Smith, Bailey and Co., Printers, 1863.

Thirty-Fifth Annual Report of the Baltimore and Ohio Railroad Co. Baltimore: William M. Innes, For the Year Ending September 30, 1861.

Thirty-Sixth Annual Report of the Baltimore and Ohio Railroad Co. Baltimore: J. B. Rose and Co., For the Year Ending September 30, 1862.

The War of the Rebellion: A Compilation of the Official Re-

cords of the Union and Confederate Armies. Washington: U. S. Government Printing Office, 1880.

Twenty-Seventh Annual Report of the Richmond, Fredericksburg and Potomac Railroad Co., May 30, 1860. Richmond: Enquirer Book and Job Press, 1860.

Twenty-Eighth Annual Report of the Richmond, Fredericksburg and Potomac Railroad Company, May 29, 1861. Richmond: Tyler, Wise and Allegre, Enquirer Book and Job Press, 1861.

Memoirs, Papers, and Personal Narratives

"A Civil War Diary From Richmond County. Diary of James M. Scates." *Northern Neck of Virginia Historical Magazine.* December, 1964.

Alexander, E. P. (General). *Military Memoirs of a Confederate.* Bloomington: Indiana University Press, 1962.

Aycock, B. L. "The Lone Star Guards." *Confederate Veteran.* February, 1923.

Basher, Roy P. (ed.). *The Collected Works of Abraham Lincoln.* Brunswick, New Jersey: Rutgers University Press, 1953.

Blake, Captain Henry N. *Three Years in the Army of the Potomac.* Boston: Lee and Shepard, 1865.

Brown, Maud. *The University Greys, Co. A. Eleventh Mississippi Regiment, Army of Northern Virginia, 1861-1865.* Richmond, Virginia: Garrett and Massie, Inc., 1940.

Butler, Benjamin F. *Butler's Book.* Boston: A. M. Thayer and Co., 1892.

Campaigns in Virginia, 1861-1862. Papers of the Military Historical Society of Massachusetts. Boston: Houghton Mifflin Co., 1895.

Cochill, Sgt. Edwin R. "The War Diary." *Bethal Baptist Church Memorial Service.* Published by Friends of Bethal Church. May, 1971.

Commager, Henry Steele. *The Blue and the Gray.* New York: The Bobbs-Merrill Co., Inc., 1950.

Cudworth, Warren H. *History of the First Regiment (Massachusetts Infantry).* Boston: Walker, Fuller and Co., 1866.

Curtis, Finley P., Jr. "The Black Shadow of the Sixties." *Confederate Veteran.* August, 1916.

Dahlgren, Madeleine (Vinton). *Memoir of John A. Dahlgren.* Boston: James R. Osgood and Co., 1882.

Davis, Nicholas A. *The Campaign from Texas to Maryland.* Richmond: Office of the Presbyterian Committee of Publications of the Confederate States, 1863.

Donald, David (ed.). *Inside Lincoln's Cabinet, The Civil War Diaries of Salmon P. Chase.* New York: Longman's, Green and Co., 1954.

Dowdey, Clifford (ed.) and Louis H. Manarin (asst. ed.). *The Wartime Papers of R. E. Lee.* Boston: Little, Brown and Co., 1961.

Dunaway, Wayland. *Reminiscences of a Rebel.* New York: The Neale Publishing Co., 1913.

Eisenschiml, Otto and Ralph Newman. *The American Iliad.* New York: The Bobbs-Merrill Co., 1947.

Fletcher, William A. *Rebel Private Front and Rear.* Austin: University of Texas Press, 1954.

French, General Samuel G. *Two Wars: An Autobiography of General Samuel G. French.* Nashville, Tenn.: Confederate Veteran, 1901.

Griggs, Earle E. (ed.) *Army Life of Frank Edwards.* La Grange, Georgia, 1911.

Hammock, John C. *With Honor Untarnished, Story of the First Arkansas Infantry Regiment.* Little Rock, Arkansas: Pioneer Press, 1961.

Hassler, William W. (ed.) *The General to His Lady, The Civil War Letters of General William Dorsey Pender to Fanny Pender.* Chapel Hill: University of North Carolina Press, 1962.

Haupt, Herman. *Reminiscences of General Herman Haupt.* Milwaukee, Wisc.: Wright & Joys Co., 1901.

Haynes, Martin A. *A History of the Second Regiment New Hampshire Volunteer Infantry in the War of the Rebellion.* Lakeport, New Hampshire, 1896.

Hesseltine, William B. (ed.) *The Tragic Conflict.* New York: George Braziller, 1962.

Hopkins, C. A. Porter (ed.). "The James J. Archer Letters." *Maryland Historical Magazine.* March, 1961.

Johnston, General Joseph E. *Narrative of Military Operations Directed During the Late War Between the States.* Bloomington: Indiana University Press, 1959.

Joinville, The Prince de. *Army of the Potomac, Its Organization, Its Commander, and Its Campaigns.* New York: Anson D. F. Randolph, 1862.

Johnson, Robert U. and Clarence C. Buel (eds.). *Battles and Leaders of the Civil War.* New York: The Century Co., 1887.

Jones, J. B. *A Rebel War Clerk's Diary.* New York: Old Hickory Bookshop, 1935.

Lamar Rifles, *A History of Company G, Eleventh Mississippi Regiment.* Roanoke, Virginia: The Stone Printing and Manufacturing Co.

Lowenfels, Walter (ed.). *Walt Whitman's Civil War.* New York: Alfred A. Knopf, 1960.

McClellan, George B. *McClellan's Own Story.* New York: Charles L. Webster and Co., 1887.

Mearns, David C. *The Lincoln Papers.* Garden City, New York: Doubleday and Co., Inc., 1948.

Nevins, Allan (ed.). *A Diary of Battle, The Personal Journals of Colonel Charles S. Wainwright, 1861-1865.* New York: Harcourt, Brace and World, Inc., 1962.

Nevins, Allan (ed.). *Diary of the Civil War, 1861-1865, George Templeton Strong.* New York: The Macmillan Co., 1962.

Nicolay, John G. and John Hay (eds.). *The Complete Works of Abraham Lincoln.* New York: Francis B. Tandy and Co., 1894.

Pierson, William W., Jr. (ed.). *Whipt'em Everytime. The Diary of Bartlett Yancey Malone.* Jackson, Tennessee: McCowat-Mercer Press, 1961.

Polley, J. B. *A Soldier's Letters to Charming Nellie.* New York: Neale Publishing Co., 1908.

Russell, Sir William Howard. *My Diary North and South.* New York: Harper, 1954.

Simpson, Harold B. *The Marshall Guards, Company E, First Texas Infantry.* Marshall, Texas: The Harrison County Historical Society, 1967.

Simpson, Harold B. (ed.). "Whip the Devil and His Hosts, The Civil War Diaries of Eugen O. Perry." *Chronicles of Smith County Texas,* VI, Fall, 1967.

Sketches of War History, 1861-1865. Military Order of the Loyal Legion of the United States, Ohio Commandery. Cincinnati: R. Clarke and Co., 1888-1896.

Sorrel, Gilbert M. *Recollection of a Confederate Staff Officer.* Jackson, Tennessee: McCowat-Mercer, 1958.

Stevens, George T. *Three Years in the Sixth Corps.* Albany: S. R. Gray Publ., 1886.

Stuart, Meriweather (ed.). "The Military Orders of Daniel Ruggles: Department of Fredericksburg, April 22-June 5, 1861." *Virginia Magazine of History and Biography,* LXIX, April, 1961.

Thompson, Robert M. and Richard Wainwright (eds.). *Confidential Correspondence of Gustavus Vasa Fox, Assistant Secretary of the Navy, 1861-1865.* New York: The DeVinne Press, 1918.

Vandiver, Frank E. (ed.). *War Memoirs, Autobiographical Sketch and Narrative of the War Between the States.* Bloomington: Indiana University Press, 1960.

Written by Participants North and South. *Annals of the War.* Philadelphia: Times Publishing Co., 1879.

Secondary Sources

Abbot, Willis J. *Blue Jackets of '61.* New York: Dodd, Mead, and Co., 1866.

Anderson, Bern. *By Sea and By River.* New York: Knopf, 1962.

Anglo, Paul M. and Earl S. Miers. *The Tragic Years, 1860-1865.* New York: Simon and Schuster, 1960.

Bates, David Homer. *Lincoln and the Telegraph Office.* New York: Appleton-Century Co., 1939.

Beitzell, Edwin W. *Life on the Potomac River.* 1968.

Bemis, Samuel Flagg. *The American Secretaries of State and Their Diplomacy.* New York: Pageant Book Co., 1958.

Benjamin, Marcus (ed.). *Washington During War Time.* Washington City: 1902.

Black, III, Robert C. *The Railroads of the Confederacy.* Chapel Hill: University of North Carolina Press, 1952.

Boynton, Charles B. *The History of the Navy During the Rebellion.* New York: D. Appleton and Co., 1867.

Brooks, Noah. *Washington in Lincoln's Time.* New York: Rinehart and Co., Inc., 1958.

Brown, George R. *Washington, A Not Too Serious History.* Baltimore: The Norman Publishing Co., 1930.

Bryan, Wilhelmus B. *A History of the National Capital.* New York: The Macmillan Co., 1916.

Buchanan, Lamont. *A Pictorial History of the Confederacy.* New York: Crown Publishers, Inc., 1951.

Carse, Robert. *Blockade, The Civil War at Sea.* New York: Rinehart and Co., Inc., 1930.

Chrismer, Wayde. "Baltimore Riot Kept Maryland in Union." *Civil War Times.* April, 1961.

Civil War Naval Chronology, 1861-1865. Washington: U. S. Government Printing Office, 1962.

Clark, Charles B. "Baltimore and the Attack on the Sixth Massachusetts Regiment, April 19, 1961." *Maryland Historical Magazine.* March, 1961.

Coggins, *Arms and Equipment of the Civil War.* Garden City, New York: Doubleday and Co., 1962.

Davis, Jefferson. *The Rise and Fall of the Confederate Government.* New York: Thomas Yoseloff, 1958.

Donald, D., J. Milhollen, M. Daplan, and H. Stuart (eds.). *Divided We Fought.* New York: The Macmillan Co., 1956.

Durkin, Joseph T. *Stephen R. Mallory:Confederate Navy Chief.* Chapel Hill: University of North Carolina Press, 1954.

Eskew, Garrett L. *Willard's of Washington.* New York: Coward-McCann, Inc., 1954.

Evans, Clement A. *Confederate Military History.* Atlanta, Georgia: Confederate Publishing Co., 1899.

Freeman, Douglas Southall. *Lee's Lieutenants, A Study in Command.* New York: Charles Scribner's Sons, 1942.

Garrison, Daniel J., Capt., U.S.N. *The Navy From Wood to Steel, 1860-1890.* New York: Franklin Watts, Inc., 1965.

Gibson, James D. "Richmond, Fredericksburg and Potomac." *Railway Progress.* August, 1947.

Gorham, George C. *Life and Public Services of Edwin M. Stanton.* New York: Houghton, Mifflin and Co., 1899.

Greeley, Horace. *The American Conflict, A History of the Great Rebellion in the United States of America, 1860-1864.* Hartford: O.D. Case and Co., 1865.

Green, Constance M. *Washington, Village and Capital, 1800-1878.* Princeton, N.J.: Princeton University Press, 1962.

Hassler, Warren W. *George B. McClellan, Shield of the Union.* Baton Rouge: Louisiana State University Press, 1957.

Haydon, F. Stansbury. *Aeronautics in the Union and Confederate Armies.* Baltimore: The Johns Hopkins Press, 1941.

Hennessy, Juliette, "The United States Army Air Arm, April 1861-April 1917." *U. S. Air Force Historical Studies Institute.* May, 1958.

Henry, Robert Selph. *The Story of the Confederacy.* New York: The Bobbs-Merrill Co., Inc., 1931.

Horan, James D. *Matthew Brady, Historian With a Camera.* New York: Bonanza Books, 1955.

Hudson, N.C. "For 116 Years the R. F. and P. Railroad has Linked the North and the South." *Traffic World.* January 3, 1953.

Jefferson Davis, A Memoir by His Wife. New York: Belford Co., 1890.

Johnston, Angus J., II. *Virginia Railroads in the Civil War.* Chapel Hill: The University of North Carolina Press, 1961.

Jones, Virgil Carrington. *The Civil War at Sea.* New York: Holt, Rinehart and Winston, 1960.

Kimmel, Stanley. *Mr. Lincoln's Washington.* New York: Coward-McCann, Inc., 1957.

La Bree, Ben (ed.). *The Confederate Soldier in the Civil War.* Paterson, New Jersey: Pageant Books, Inc., 1959.

Leech, Margaret. *Reveille in Washington, 1860-1865.* New York: Gosset and Dunlap, 1941.

Lossing, Benson J. *A History of the Civil War.* New York: The War Memorial Association, 1912.

Lossing, Benson J. *Pictorial History of the Civil War in the United States of America.* Philadelphia: George W. Childs, Publisher, 1866.

Lord, Dr. Francis A. "Both Sides Used Torpedoes Widely." *Civil War Times.* January, 1964.

Lord, Dr. Francis A. "The United States Military Railroad Service." *Civil War Times.* October, 1962.

Lord, Dr. Francis A. "U. S. Balloon Corps' Potential Unrealized." *Civil War Times.* June, 1961.

Mahan, A. T. *The Gulf and Inland Waters.* New York: Jack Brussel, 1959.

Merrill, James M. *The Rebel Shore.* Boston: Little, Brown and Co., 1957.

Miller, Francis T. (ed.). *The Photographic History of the Civil War.* New York: The Review of Reviews Co., 1912.

Moat, Louis S. (ed.). *Frank Leslie's Illustrated Famous Leaders and Battle Scenes of the Civil War.* New York: Mrs. Frank Leslie, Publ., 1896.

Mordecai, John B. *A Brief History of the Richmond, Fredericksburg and Potomac Railroad.* February, 1940.

Nichols, James L. *Confederate Engineers.* Tuscaloosa, Ala.: Confederate Publishing Co., Inc., 1957.

Paris, The Comte de. *History of the Civil War in America.* Philadelphia: J. H. Coates, 1875.

Plum, William R. *The Military Telegraph During the Civil War in the United States.* Chicago: Jansen, McClurg and Co., 1882.

Pollard, Edward A. *The First Year of the War.* Richmond: West and Johnston, 1862.

Porter, Adm. David D. *The Naval History of the Civil War.* New York: The Sherman Publishing Co., 1886.

Proctor, John C. *Washington, Past and Present.* New York: Lewis Historical Publishing Co., Inc., 1930.

Rawlings, James Scott. *Virginia's Colonial Churches.* Richmond: Garrett and Massie, 1963.

Roberts, Chalmers M. *Washington, Past and Present.* Washington, D. C.: Public Affairs Press, 1949-1950.

Ropes, John C. *The Story of the Civil War.* New York: G. P. Putman's Sons, 1933.

Scharf, J. Thomas. *History of the Confederate States Navy.* New York: Rogers and Sherwood, 1887.

Simpson, Harold B. *Hood's Texas Brigade:Lee's Grenadier Guard.* Waco, Texas: Texian Press, 1970.

Soley, James Russell. *The Blockade and the Cruisers.* New York: Jack Brussel Publ., 1959.

Stepp, John W. and I. W. Hill (eds.). *Mirror of the War, The Washington Star Reports the Civil War.* Englewood Cliffs, N.J.: Prentice Hall, Inc., 1961.

Stern, Philip Van Doren. *The Confederate Navy: A Pictorial History.* Garden City, N.Y.: Doubleday and Co., 1962.

Summers, Festus P. "The Baltimore and Ohio—First in War." *Civil War History.* September, 1961.

Templeman, Eleanor Lee. *Arlington Heritage,* 1959.

Templeman, Eleanor Lee. *Northern Virginia Heritage,* 1966.

The American Soldier in the Civil War, A Pictorial History of the Campaigns and Conflicts of the War Between the States. New York: Bryon, Taylor and Co., 1895.

The R. F. & P. *Yesterday and Today.*

The Symbol and the Sword, Washington, D. C., 1860-1865. The District of Columbia Centennial Commission, 1962.

Turner, Charles W. "The Richmond, Fredericksburg, and Potomac, 1861-1865." *Civil War History.* September, 1961.

Turner, George W. *Victory Rode the Rails.* New York: The Bobbs-Merrill Co., Inc., 1953.

Wariner, N. E. (compiled by). *A Register of Military Events in Virginia, 1861-1865.* Virginia Civil War Commission, 1959.

Weber, Thomas. *The Northern Railroads in the Civil War, 1861-1865.* New York: King's County Press, Columbia University, 1952.

West Point Atlas of the Civil War. New York: Frederick A. Praeger, 1962.

Weigley, Frank Russell. *Quartermaster-General of the Union Army.* New York: Columbia University Press, 1959.

Weigley, Russell F. "Montgomery Meigs—A Personality Profile." *Civil War Times.* November, 1964.

Whyte, James H. "The Unquiet Potomac." *Civil War Times.* December, 1960.

Williams, Kenneth P. *Lincoln Finds a General: A Military Study of the Civil War.* New York: The Macmillan Co., 1949-1959.

Wilson, John L. *Battles of America by Sea and Land.* New York: Patterson and Neilson, 1878.

Wilstach, Paul. *Potomac Landings.* Indianapolis: The Bobbs-Merrill Co., 1920.

Wooster, Ralph A. "The Membership of the Maryland Legislature of 1861." *Maryland Historical Magazine.* March, 1961.

Wright, M., B. LaBree and J. Boyd (eds.). *Official and Illustrated War Record.* Washington, D. C.: 1898.

Newspapers

Daily National Intelligencer

Fredericksburg News

Harper's Weekly

Leslie's Illustrated Weekly

New York Herald

New York Tribune

Richmond Examiner

The Illustrated London News

The Washington Star

INDEX

189